OPPOSING
VIEWPOINTS®
SERIES

D0126645

Veterans

Other Books of Related Interest:

Opposing Viewpoints Series

Afghanistan

The Aging Population

US Foreign Policy

World Peace

At Issue Series

Biological and Chemical Weapons

Drones

Do Veterans Receive Adequate Health Care?

How Should the Armed Forces Address the Casualties of War?

Current Controversies Series

Military Families

The Elderly

Gays in the Military

Patriotism

"Congress shall make no law ... abridging the freedom of speech, or of the press."

First Amendment to the US Constitution

The basic foundation of our democracy is the First Amendment guarantee of freedom of expression. The Opposing Viewpoints series is dedicated to the concept of this basic freedom and the idea that it is more important to practice it than to enshrine it.

Veterans

Dedria Bryfonski, Book Editor

GREENHAVEN PRESS
A part of Gale, Cengage Learning

GALE
CENGAGE Learning·

Farmington Hills, Mich • San Francisco • New York • Waterville, Maine
Meriden, Conn • Mason, Ohio • Chicago

Patricia Coryell, *Vice President & Publisher, New Products & GVRL*
Douglas Dentino, *Manager, New Products*
Judy Galens, *Acquisitions Editor*

For more information, contact:
Greenhaven Press
27500 Drake Rd.
Farmington Hills, MI 48331-3535
Or you can visit our Internet site at gale.cengage.com

For product information and technology assistance, contact us at

Gale Customer Support, 1-800-877-4253
For permission to use material from this text or product, submit all requests online at www.cengage.com/permissions

Further permissions questions can be emailed to permissionrequest@cengage.com

Articles in Greenhaven Press anthologies are often edited for length to meet page requirements. In addition, original titles of these works are changed to clearly present the main thesis and to explicitly indicate the author's opinion. Every effort is made to ensure that Greenhaven Press accurately reflects the original intent of the authors. Every effort has been made to trace the owners of copyrighted material.

Cover Image © Plume Photography/Shutterstock.com.

LIBRARY OF CONGRESS CATALOGING-IN-PUBLICATION DATA

Veterans / Dedria Bryfonski, book editor.
     pages cm. -- (Opposing viewpoints)
  Includes bibliographical references and index.
     ISBN 978-0-7377-7298-2 (hardcover) -- ISBN 978-0-7377-7299-9 (pbk.)
  1. Veterans--United States. 2. Veterans--Services for--United States--Juvenile literature. 3. Veterans--United States--Social conditions--Juvenile literature. 4. United States. Department of Veterans Affairs--Juvenile literature. I. Bryfonski, Dedria.
     UB357.V376 2015
     362.860973--dc23
                            2014044676

Printed in Mexico
1 2 3 4 5 6 7 19 18 17 16 15

Contents

Chapter 3: Does the Department of Veterans Affairs Effectively Help Veterans?

Chapter 4: How Effective Are the Government's Education Programs for Veterans?

Why Consider Opposing Viewpoints?

> "The only way in which a human being can make some approach to knowing the whole of a subject is by hearing what can be said about it by persons of every variety of opinion and studying all modes in which it can be looked at by every character of mind. No wise man ever acquired his wisdom in any mode but this."
>
> John Stuart Mill

In our media-intensive culture it is not difficult to find differing opinions. Thousands of newspapers and magazines and dozens of radio and television talk shows resound with differing points of view. The difficulty lies in deciding which opinion to agree with and which "experts" seem the most credible. The more inundated we become with differing opinions and claims, the more essential it is to hone critical reading and thinking skills to evaluate these ideas. Opposing Viewpoints books address this problem directly by presenting stimulating debates that can be used to enhance and teach these skills. The varied opinions contained in each book examine many different aspects of a single issue. While examining these conveniently edited opposing views, readers can develop critical thinking skills such as the ability to compare and contrast authors' credibility, facts, argumentation styles, use of persuasive techniques, and other stylistic tools. In short, the Opposing Viewpoints Series is an ideal way to attain the higher-level thinking and reading skills so essential in a culture of diverse and contradictory opinions.

In addition to providing a tool for critical thinking, Opposing Viewpoints books challenge readers to question their own strongly held opinions and assumptions. Most people form their opinions on the basis of upbringing, peer pressure, and personal, cultural, or professional bias. By reading carefully balanced opposing views, readers must directly confront new ideas as well as the opinions of those with whom they disagree. This is not to argue simplistically that everyone who reads opposing views will—or should—change his or her opinion. Instead, the series enhances readers' understanding of their own views by encouraging confrontation with opposing ideas. Careful examination of others' views can lead to the readers' understanding of the logical inconsistencies in their own opinions, perspective on why they hold an opinion, and the consideration of the possibility that their opinion requires further evaluation.

Evaluating Other Opinions

To ensure that this type of examination occurs, Opposing Viewpoints books present all types of opinions. Prominent spokespeople on different sides of each issue as well as well-known professionals from many disciplines challenge the reader. An additional goal of the series is to provide a forum for other, less known, or even unpopular viewpoints. The opinion of an ordinary person who has had to make the decision to cut off life support from a terminally ill relative, for example, may be just as valuable and provide just as much insight as a medical ethicist's professional opinion. The editors have two additional purposes in including these less known views. One, the editors encourage readers to respect others' opinions—even when not enhanced by professional credibility. It is only by reading or listening to and objectively evaluating others' ideas that one can determine whether they are worthy of consideration. Two, the inclusion of such viewpoints encourages the important critical thinking skill of objectively evaluating an author's credentials and bias. This evaluation will illuminate an author's reasons for taking a particular stance on an issue and will aid in readers' evaluation of the author's ideas.

It is our hope that these books will give readers a deeper understanding of the issues debated and an appreciation of the complexity of even seemingly simple issues when good and honest people disagree. This awareness is particularly important in a democratic society such as ours in which people enter into public debate to determine the common good. Those with whom one disagrees should not be regarded as enemies but rather as people whose views deserve careful examination and may shed light on one's own.

Thomas Jefferson once said that "difference of opinion leads to inquiry, and inquiry to truth." Jefferson, a broadly educated man, argued that "if a nation expects to be ignorant and free ... it expects what never was and never will be." As individuals and as a nation, it is imperative that we consider the opinions of others and examine them with skill and discernment. The Opposing Viewpoints series is intended to help readers achieve this goal.

David L. Bender and Bruno Leone,
Founders

Introduction

> *"For their service and sacrifice, warm words of thanks from a grateful nation are more than warranted, but they aren't nearly enough. We also owe our veterans the care they were promised and the benefits that they have earned. . . . But we know that for too long, we've fallen short of meeting that commitment. Too many wounded warriors go without the care that they need. Too many veterans don't receive the support that they've earned. Too many who once wore our nation's uniform now sleep in our nation's streets."*
>
> *—Barack Obama,*
> *March 19, 2009*

It's a familiar sight at major league baseball parks across the nation: the game-starting baseball delivered to the mound by a soldier fresh from military duty while those in attendance stand and cheer. Throughout the summer of 2014, the Iraq and Afghanistan Veterans of America held parades in communities around the country to pay tribute to veterans of these wars. "Thank you for your service" is a phrase returning veterans hear frequently at public and private events. All of this is in stark contrast to the often hostile reception Vietnam veterans received in the late 1960s and early 1970s. ROTC instructor Tim Hsia writing in the *New York Times* said that this is "perhaps the most pro-veteran environment in decades."

At the end of 2013, there were 21.9 million US veterans— 2.6 million of them veterans of the wars in Afghanistan and Iraq. The vast majority of veterans adjust successfully to civilian life, many aided by the array of benefits made available to assist them with education, employment, health care, and vocational training.

However, for some veterans, the transition to civilian life does not go smoothly. According to Jimmy DeFoor, veterans services officer for Taylor County in Kansas, as quoted in a November 2012 article in the *Abilene Reporter-News*:

> The major challenge our veterans are facing is trying to re-integrate back into society. They're facing problems like (difficulty in) finding jobs, which is a major issue, because if you can't find a job, oftentimes that leads to homelessness.
>
> Many of them are suffering from post-traumatic stress disorder and that's something they need to overcome. A lot of them also have traumatic brain injury.

Among the most troubling statistic is the number of homeless veterans—fifty-eight thousand of them in January 2013, the US Department of Housing and Urban Development estimated, approximately 12 percent of the total homeless population. According to law professor Steven K. Berenson in a *Family Law Quarterly* article in the summer of 2011, "Simply put, it is unconscionable that people who have often sacrificed a great deal in service to their country should face such deplorable circumstances upon their return to the home front." According to the US Department of Veterans Affairs (VA), 92 percent of homeless veterans are men, with the majority being single, living in an urban area, and many suffering from mental illness, alcoholism, or substance abuse.

There are a number of reasons why veterans become homeless. According to Green Doors, a Texas-based nonprofit whose mission is to help the homeless, the greatest risk factors for veteran homelessness are a lack of support and social isolation after discharge. Berenson details some of the conditions that can result in veteran homelessness:

> Many veterans find the transition from the structure and fast pace of military life back to the relatively unstructured

and slower pace of civilian life to be difficult. Large numbers of veterans also suffer from mental health issues, including post-traumatic stress disorder (PTSD), traumatic brain injuries (TBI), and major depression. The pervasiveness of these maladies among veterans returning from the current conflicts in Iraq and Afghanistan is particularly high. Even under the best of circumstances, these illnesses can be difficult to diagnose. Combining that fact with a military culture that frowns on admitting weakness and seeking out help means that many veterans suffering from these illnesses will not receive a proper diagnosis. And even for those veterans with proper diagnoses, accessing available resources to deal with these issues can be difficult.

In 2009, President Barack Obama and then secretary of veterans affairs Eric Shinseki announced a goal of ending homelessness among veterans by 2015. As of January 2014, homelessness had been reduced by 24 percent since 2010. A key feature of the initiative was a $600 million grant for community-based programs and nonprofits to provide services to very low-income veteran families. Some advocates for veterans, including John Driscoll, president of the National Coalition for Homeless Veterans, praise the program, but feel that the goal is overly optimistic. He explains in a November 2013 article in *Stars and Stripes* that "we may have to reexamine what success is. Programs are headed in the right direction. But we're only beginning to see what the real demand for services will be for the younger veterans. I think 2015 was an ambitious goal."

Although progress is being made in reducing the number of homeless veterans, homelessness remains one of the issues facing today's veterans.

The authors of the viewpoints presented in *Opposing Viewpoints: Veterans* explore the issues and challenges facing veterans in chapters titled "Is Unemployment Among Veterans a Serious Issue?," "How Can Suicide Among Veterans Be Prevented?," "Does the Department of Veterans Affairs Effectively

Help Veterans?," and "How Effective Are the Government's Education Programs for Veterans?" The information contained in this volume provides insight into some of the recent controversies surrounding the VA and health care for veterans, as well as offers some suggestions on how to improve employment and education benefits for veterans and how to reduce veteran suicide.

**OPPOSING
VIEWPOINTS®
SERIES**

CHAPTER 1

Is Unemployment Among Veterans a Serious Issue?

Chapter Preface

Although the unemployment rate for veterans is similar to that of the civilian population, the unemployment rate for post-9/11 veterans, or those veterans in active-duty service after September 11, 2001, is higher than that of other veterans and the general population.

According to October 2014 numbers from the Bureau of Labor Statistics (BLS), the unemployment rate of the civilian population was 5.8 percent, compared to 4.5 percent for all veterans over the age of eighteen. The unemployment rate of post-9/11 veterans was 7.2 percent. Since there are 2.8 million post-9/11 veterans out of a total veteran population of 21.8 million, unemployment among this group has been a matter of national concern and public policy. Particularly hard hit are female post-9/11 veterans, with an unemployment rate of 11.2 percent, according to the BLS.

In order to address the issue of female veteran unemployment, it is important to understand the reasons why this group has a harder time transitioning to civilian employment. According to journalist Meena Thiruvengadam in a February 17, 2011, article in *USA Today*, "No one can pinpoint exactly why the transition to the civilian workplace seems tougher for female veterans, but researchers and advocacy groups point toward a Veterans Affairs system that doesn't adequately meet women's health care, child care, and psychological needs; a tendency among women to serve as a primary caregiver for children; and a civilian sector that may not fully understand the role of women in the military."

John E. Pickens III, executive director of VeteransPlus, a nonprofit counseling service for veterans, cites the unique challenges facing female veterans seeking employment. He said in an article at NBCNews.com that "more women were deployed than ever before but an awful lot of them are single moms who face the challenge of coming home. Someone has been taking care of their kids, and now they want to refocus their lives on being mom. Often, though, the kind of employment that may be available to them is not sufficient to meet that dream of both working and being that stable mom."

According to Dr. Irene Trowell-Harris, director of the US Department of Veterans Affairs (VA) Center for Women Veterans, contributing to the high rate of unemployment for female veterans is the reality that many of them do not consider themselves veterans, because they did not serve in combat, and therefore, they don't apply for the benefits that could help them find employment. Trowell-Harris cites a national survey conducted by the VA that found that 31 percent of female veterans did not think they were eligible for VA benefits.

Another factor contributing to unemployment among female veterans is the prevalence of military sexual trauma (MST). According to Margret Bell, a member of the MST support team for the VA, about one in five women reveal to their VA health care provider that they were sexually assaulted while in the military. Since sexual trauma tends to be underreported, she states, the true number is probably significantly higher. Among the mental health disorders caused by MST are post-traumatic stress disorder, depression, anxiety, substance abuse, and psychoses. According to Bell, among the problems associated with these mental health disorders is difficulty finding and maintaining employment.

The problem of female veteran unemployment is one that the US government and veterans' advocacy organizations are seeking to solve. In the following chapter, commentators, journalists, and politicians debate a variety of issues surrounding unemployment among veterans.

> *"The fact is that once most veterans get into the workplace, they do extremely well and the statistics show that their overall unemployment rates are lower than their civilian counterparts."*

Most Veterans Transition Successfully into Civilian Jobs

G.I. Jobs

G.I. Jobs is a magazine aimed at people transitioning out of military service and seeking civilian career training and jobs. In the following viewpoint, the editors argue that there has been a disproportionate amount of attention paid to the fluctuating unemployment rates of post-9/11 veterans, creating the inaccurate impression that veterans have a hard time finding jobs. The reality is that the jobless rate for veterans has been lower than that for civilians for every year since 2000. The editors assert that although it is true that the unemployment rate of younger veterans is higher than that of civilians, several factors make the jobless rate of veterans appear worse than it really is.

As you read, consider the following questions:

1. According to the viewpoint, what was the annual average unemployment rate for all veterans in 2010 and what was the average unemployment rate of the general population?

2. What are four factors that skew the unemployment rate of young veterans, according to the viewpoint?

3. According to Matt Rose, what are some of the assets that a military background brings to corporate jobs?

Chris Volk isn't the kind of soldier you usually see on TV. The 26-year-old Operation Iraqi Freedom [OIF] veteran served in a combat zone, fixing HVAC [heating, ventilating, and air-conditioning] equipment in a maintenance battalion. Volk used his education benefits when he left the army to earn an associate degree, then landed an apprenticeship with Ameren Illinois, a subsidiary of Ameren Corporation. In June [2011] he'll move up to gas utility journeyman—a good job with good benefits.

There's nothing sensational about Volk's success story. He's not recovering from combat wounds, he's not suffering from PTSD [post-traumatic stress disorder], he's not homeless and he's not coping with TBI [traumatic brain injury]. Volk made a smooth transition to civilian life, but stories like his don't get much attention.

Yet Volk represents the vast majority of America's veterans—including the 2 million who served in Iraq and Afghanistan. Their stories of success transitioning from the military to companies and campuses have been told in every issue of *G.I. Jobs* magazine for the past 10 years. You'll find them on the covers, you'll find them on the pages inside and you'll find them leading quiet, productive lives in cities and towns across America.

The stories that get told about veterans usually focus on the small percentage that are struggling to find jobs or dealing with other serious issues. Although unintended, this focus skews the public's perception and creates a misperception that can hurt the job prospects for all veterans.

Perception Is Not Reality

Much has been made of the unemployment rates for the veterans who served after Sept. 11, 2001—particularly those between the ages of 18 and 24. Stories about these veterans' unemployment rates, which fluctuate considerably from month to month, follow each new release of data by the U.S. Bureau of Labor Statistics (BLS). Such attention creates the misperception that returning veterans can't find jobs. The reality is that even the youngest veterans, many of whom voluntarily take longer to enter the job market, excel once they are employed because of the skills—both tangible and intangible—they learned in the military.

"The fact is that once most veterans get into the workplace, they do extremely well and the statistics show that their overall unemployment rates are lower than their civilian counterparts," said Charles S. "Chick" Ciccolella, president of CSC Group LLC and former assistant secretary for Veterans' Employment and Training Service (VETS).

The annual average unemployment rate for ALL veterans in 2010 stood at 8.7 percent compared to the general population at 9.4 percent. That is not an anomaly.

"If you look at the annual unemployment rates over the last 20 or 30 years, the rates for veterans are lower than for nonveterans," Ciccolella said. "For example, in 2009 the unemployment rate for nonveterans was 9.3 percent, while the rate for veterans overall was 8.1 percent."

In fact, the jobless rate for all veterans was lower than nonveterans every year since 2000—even through two recessions.

What About the Young Vets?

Younger workers have had the highest unemployment rates since Sept. 11 [2001], both among veterans and nonveterans. The jobless rate for veterans ages 18 to 24 was 20.6 percent in 2010, according to the BLS, compared to nonveterans at 17.3. But a look behind the numbers indicates they may appear worse than they really are. There are several reasons the unemployment rates for young veterans may be skewed.

Reason 1: Comp Time, SIR!

Many veterans in the 18- to 24-year-old age group have been forward deployed three, four or five times during their short military careers. When they separate, they often choose to take some time off before going to work or school.

"After such a demanding deployment schedule, what veteran wouldn't want to take advantage of 60 days of basket leave and an ability to collect unemployment for a while in an effort to recharge their batteries prior to starting a civilian career?" said Chris Hale, president of the National Veteran-Owned Business Association (NaVOBA). "Most civilians need comp time for working an occasional Saturday. Veterans are simply looking for a little comp time for being forward deployed for 12 months straight. Can you blame them?"

Ciccolella agrees. "Some veterans I have talked to want to take a break after service before they get into the workforce or go back to school," he said. "I think that is very normal."

While this time off is richly deserved, it inflates the unemployment rate for America's youngest veterans.

Reason 2: Return to Hometown

Many young veterans leaving the military haven't decided what to do next. "This could be because they've been so busy in the military that they may not have had enough time to really think about what they will do when they leave the service," Ciccolella said.

Some return to their hometowns to explore their options.

"Many veterans joined the service because there were no jobs in their hometown," said Hale, a nine-year navy veteran. "Some veterans who choose to return to those hometowns after the military find that the job prospects haven't improved. It takes some veterans a little time to exhaust that hometown dream before migrating to places with better job prospects."

In the meantime, these young veterans, too, are on the unemployment rolls.

Reason 3: Back to School

Tens of thousands of young veterans take advantage of the Post-9/11 GI Bill [Post-9/11 Veterans Educational Assistance Act] to go to college. According to the U.S. Department of Veterans Affairs (VA), more than 440,000 veterans or family members have used the new GI Bill since it was enacted in 2009. But even before the Post-9/11 GI Bill, 15 percent of veterans between the ages of 18 and 24 enrolled in college in the first month after separation from the military, according to the BLS, which tracked the transition of veterans from 1998 to 2008. Two years after separating, nearly a quarter of veterans ages 18 to 24 were enrolled in college.

Those who took their time enrolling were likely collecting unemployment while they decided what to study and where to go to school. Veterans also can collect unemployment while they research schools, apply to schools and wait for classes to start—a process that can take months. This also drives up the unemployment rate for America's youngest veterans.

Reason 4: Delayed by Deployment

Regardless of how skewed the unemployment numbers are, there's no question America's youngest veterans face a tough job market when they transition out of the military. For those who enlisted right out of high school and are embarking on their first job search, deployments can deter their preparation for a civilian career.

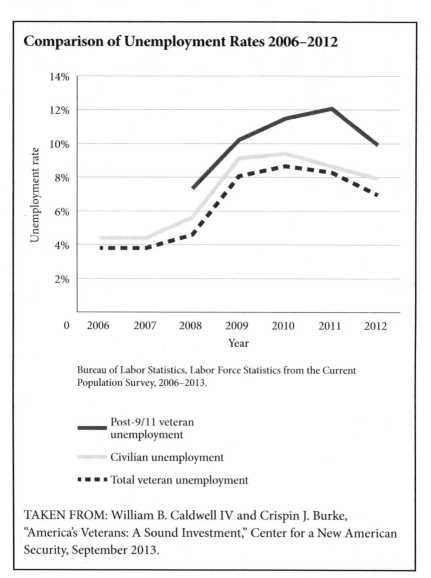

Comparison of Unemployment Rates 2006–2012

Bureau of Labor Statistics, Labor Force Statistics from the Current Population Survey, 2006–2013.

——— Post-9/11 veteran unemployment

——— Civilian unemployment

■ ■ ■ Total veteran unemployment

TAKEN FROM: William B. Caldwell IV and Crispin J. Burke, "America's Veterans: A Sound Investment," Center for a New American Security, September 2013.

Bill McMillian, transition services manager at Fort Bragg, N.C., oversees the Army Career and Alumni Program (ACAP) that helps 400 to 500 soldiers a month prepare for their military-to-civilian transition. He said veterans returning from Iraq and Afghanistan often don't have time to properly prepare for their transition. Soldiers frequently return from deployment with 60 days or less until they separate. Two to four weeks might be spent on leave getting reacquainted with their families, leaving little time for a proper job search.

"So they're out of here before they can take advantage of the programs for them," said McMillian, a 20-year army veteran. "There's a lot of things going on that are causing the unemployment rates to go where they are."

The op tempo of the Post-9/11 era caught up to Rob Wells, 31. The former army captain and OIF veteran had set a separation date in 2006 when he was "stop-lossed," forcing him to postpone his transition plans. "I was actually approved to leave two weeks before my separation date," Wells said. "I had no plan and no time to get one together."

Wells briefly sold cars—a job he hated—just to pay his bills. After losing a job as a financial advisor trainee in 2008, Wells found a civilian career he loves working as a human resources supervisor for Fluor Corporation.

"I should have started planning at least a year in advance, that way my stop-loss wouldn't have hurt as much," Wells said. "I would have thought about what I wanted to do and where I wanted to live."

Key to Success

The unemployment numbers for all veterans confirm that once America's youngest veterans set a career course, most excel because of their military training. That's no secret to corporate America.

"Those who wear our nation's uniforms are mission-focused, highly skilled, motivated and possess unique experiences and technical knowledge," said Matt Rose, chairman, president and chief executive officer for BNSF Railway. "Military candidates embody the core competencies of BNSF: leadership, teamwork and the ability to perform safely in a fast-paced, dynamic environment."

Corporate America Heavily Recruits Vets

The corporate horizon is lined with companies that invest heavily in recruiting military veterans. Thousands of companies compete fiercely each year to be named to the *G.I. Jobs* magazine Top 100 Military Friendly Employers list, which honors the companies that are doing the most to recruit America's veterans.

"Active military duty has graduated beyond the traditional combat-only responsibilities to include the hands-on application of leading-edge technologies, logistics, communications, analysis and leadership—skills in high demand at ManTech," said Carlos S. Echalar, vice president of human resources for ManTech International. Half of the company's 9,700 employees are veterans. . . . "Veterans who possess these skills closely match our customer base and have a deeper understanding of our customers' infrastructure, culture and customs."

Write Your Own Success Story

Every year *G.I. Jobs* magazine charts the best practices of the Top 100 Military Friendly Employers. This year's report reveals that:

- 92 percent of the top 100 employers had at least one hiring manager devoted to recruiting military veterans, up from 90 percent last year.

- The companies on the 2011 list reported an average of 23 percent of their new hires were military veterans, up from 20 percent in 2010.

- 78 percent pay the difference between military salary and civilian salary for members of the guard and reserve who are deployed, up from 71 percent in 2010.

So don't be discouraged if you're getting ready for your own military-to-civilian transition—despite what you might hear. America's employers get it. Just ask Chris Volk.

"The data over the past few years indicate that veterans have struggled to find their place in a sluggish civilian economy."

Undervalued and Underemployed

Andrew Tilghman

Andrew Tilghman is a staff writer for Army Times. *In the following viewpoint, he argues that many young veterans are finding it difficult to obtain meaningful employment following their military service. Even after taking advantage of training and education made possible by the Post-9/11 GI Bill, many are settling for low-paying jobs, he contends. The federal government has recognized the importance of reducing unemployment and underemployment among veterans and has responded with a variety of initiatives and programs, Tilghman reports.*

As you read, consider the following questions:

1. According to the viewpoint, what was the unemployment rate of young veterans in 2011 compared to the unemployment rate of civilians?

2. In what ways do unemployed veterans differ from un-employed civilians, according to Tilghman?

3. According to Tilghman, what are some of the programs the federal government is introducing to reduce veteran unemployment?

Like many veterans, former sailor Nick Walker has struggled to find direction since leaving the military in 2008.

Initially, the former yeoman second class returned to his home state of Indiana—30th among the states in unemploy-ment—and started school. Using the GI Bill, he spent several years as a full-time student, studying psychology.

After graduating in 2011, he looked for a job—any job. He applied to restaurants, retail stores, a medical supply company and a pawn shop.

Earlier this year [2012], after months of leaning on his parents to help with his cell phone bill, he finally took the only job offer he got: The 28-year-old college graduate and military veteran now works at a Burger King.

"I'm finally getting 40 hours a week, and they're looking to make me manager soon," he said in a recent interview.

Walker's experience echoes that of thousands of veterans across the country in recent years: separation from the mili-tary followed by a mixture of government benefits and school—often in a field with limited real-world potential—a bout with unemployment and, finally, a job that may fall far short of hopes and expectations.

Last year, the unemployment rate for the youngest veter-ans hit a startling high of more than 15 percent—roughly one in seven—and it has remained persistently higher than civilian rates of unemployment.

Statistics sometimes suggest the situation is improving; this summer, the jobless rate for those young veterans, bu-reaucratically known as Gulf War II veterans, dropped to 8.9

percent, higher than the overall civilian unemployment rate of 8.3 percent but close enough to be what experts call "statistically insignificant."

Yet by October, the gap had widened once more. Gulf War II veterans reported a jobless rate of about 10 percent, far higher than the nation's overall rate, which had dropped to 7.9 percent.

Some experts say the monthly rates can fluctuate significantly because the veterans' sample size is quite small. But monthly ups and downs aside, the data over the past few years indicate that veterans have struggled to find their place in a sluggish civilian economy.

That's become a problem for the White House, the Pentagon and lawmakers in both parties, who face sweeping criticism that a nation sending troops into combat overseas too often fails to help them find gainful employment when they return home.

"The services have realized it's in their long-term interests to take care of people and prepare them for getting out," said Patrick Bellon, the executive director of Veterans for Common Sense. "They really can't afford to have the public perceive the military as a dead-end option. That could be a real threat to the all-volunteer force."

Such concerns have prompted a government-wide effort to boost veterans' employment. But the impact that government can have on this issue remains unclear.

The Student Track

Many out-of-work veterans bear scant resemblance to traditional unemployed civilians. For one thing, roughly one-third of "jobless" vets are in school, government data show.

Most likely, they are tapping GI Bill benefits and collecting a living stipend from the Veterans Affairs Department.

"People are coming out of the military and making a decision about whether they want to go into the labor market or go back to school, and a lot are choosing to do both," said Jim Borbely, an economist who studies veterans' employment trends at the Labor Department. "They go to school on the GI Bill, and take advantage of all the benefits available to them by taking unemployment at the same time. They are not who we typically think of when we talk about the unemployed."

In fact, some veterans see their generous Post-9/11 GI Bill [Post-9/11 Veterans Educational Assistance Act] benefits as a way to expressly avoid—or at least put off—the imperative to find a job.

Ryan Dirksen, a 32-year-old former marine who lives with his wife and son near Modesto, Calif., found a way to collect a super-sized housing stipend along with his tuition benefits while he studies business management.

Instead of enrolling at his local community college, he climbed into his Toyota Camry twice a week for a four-hour round-trip commute across California's San Joaquin Valley and San Francisco Bay to attend the Community College of San Francisco [CCSF].

Dirksen stayed on the roster at CCSF essentially for one reason: the Post-9/11 GI Bill housing stipend, which is pegged to the military's basic allowance for housing [BAH] rate for a married E-5 [sergeant] in the zip code for the location of the student veteran's school.

As a CCSF student, Dirksen's housing stipend was based on the BAH rate for the central San Francisco area, which is the highest in the nation at $2,742 per month—far more than the roughly $1,200 a month he would have received if his stipend had been based on the BAH rate for Modesto Junior College near his home.

"It makes a huge difference," Dirksen said. "I have a wife and child . . . to support."

He continued to take some classes at Modesto Junior College, but says, "It was in my best interest to make sure that I

Employers Unwilling to Hire in Uncertain Economy

Capt. Mike Bolton moved through the hundreds gathered at the convention center with a black binder of 41 résumés. It was yet another veterans' job fair. Bolton's job is to help his fellow Army National Guard soldiers find careers after their combat tours. . . .

Everyone says they want to hire veterans. . . .

Here in Oklahoma, Bolton knows better. When hiring managers flip through his binder of résumés, they aren't thinking about whether the nation has an obligation to its combat veterans. They are weighing whether they can really afford to take on one more employee in this uncertain economy, whether it makes sense to wait just a few more months.

Greg Jaffe, "After Decade of War, Troops Still Struggling to Find Work," Washington Post, *March 19, 2013.*

maintained at least one course on [the CCSF] campus there so I could receive the full [BAH] benefits."

After two years of that commuting routine, Dirksen transferred to George Washington University in Washington, D.C.

The GI Bill offers veterans like Dirksen a valuable—even lucrative—option that is not available to unemployed civilians.

"There are jobs out there, but a lot of the pay is very low," said Jarom Vahai, a former marine who helps veterans in the San Francisco area through a group called Green Careers for Veterans. "If these jobs are not going to pay more than a veteran can get just by staying in school, then you're not going to see veterans show up for these jobs."

Government Steps Up

Despite the effects of the Post-9/11 GI Bill, there is little question that the veterans' unemployment problem is real.

Efforts to reduce joblessness among vets have garnered a level of bipartisan support that is rare in today's polarized political climate, with many new ideas, initiatives and programs popping up in recent years.

For example, the Departments of Defense, Veterans Affairs, Labor and Education are in the midst of a broad overhaul of the Transition Assistance Program [TAP] that supports troops separating from the military.

TAP was once a voluntary seminar lasting a few hours and offering rudimentary tips on such things as how to access post-service benefits. Many troops simply skipped it.

The new program involves two to three days of mandatory core counseling that covers real-world skills such as résumé writing, translating military acronyms for potential civilian employers, and suggested dress codes for job interviews. The program also offers specialized instruction for troops with specific plans to attend college or start a small business.

The new version of TAP is being tested at seven locations, with plans to expand the new courses force-wide in 2013.

The effort signals a cultural shift within the Pentagon. For years, many senior leaders quietly feared that preparing service members to succeed in the civilian job market might hurt military retention.

Now, however, helping troops get on the right track as they separate is viewed as a key mission. That's fueled in part by budget concerns as the Defense Department [DoD] is on track to spend more than $1 billion on unemployment benefits for recently separated and out-of-work veterans, more than double the cost before the recession in 2008, according to DoD data.

On Capitol Hill, lawmakers have passed a flurry of new laws aimed at making it easier for veterans to find work. For example, a law that took effect in August requires federal agencies to accept military experience to fulfill training requirements for federal licenses, potentially expediting jobs in such fields as aircraft maintenance and communications.

Another law passed in late 2011 gives employers a tax credit for hiring veterans and allows troops to apply for federal jobs even before they leave service. That ends the long-time practice of requiring troops to provide separation papers as part of the application process.

The White House also has targeted the private sector. In an effort led by First Lady Michelle Obama, the administration's Joining Forces campaign has targeted thousands of private sector companies and business groups and urged them to hire veterans. White House officials say more than 2,000 companies have signed up and hired more than 125,000 veterans.

The Joining Forces initiative may be one of the best models for addressing veterans' employment concerns, said John McKinny, a recently retired veteran employment specialist with the Labor Department in Texas.

"These guys are coming home to the worst economy since the Great Depression," McKinny said. "The most effective thing we can do is educate the employer community and say, 'Look, these are great young men and women.' And once they get hired, employers will realize that. But changes like that may not manifest in a week or two . . . or even a year."

> *"The skills gained in the military are directly transferable to many of the positions being sought to be filled by the federal government."*

Veterans Receive Preference in Hiring for Federal Jobs

Barbara A. Adams

Barbara A. Adams is the president and chief executive officer of CareerProPlus.com and is considered an industry expert for military transition to civilian employment. In the following viewpoint, she argues that there are many strong reasons for veterans to consider applying for federal jobs. The federal government has many positions opening up, as over half of the current workforce will be eligible for retirement within the next few years, she states. Furthermore, Adams explains, the federal government values military experience for positions in the Department of Homeland Security, the Federal Bureau of Investigation (FBI), and the Central Intelligence Agency (CIA). Many veterans are eligible to have five to ten points added to their application score, giving them an advantage over their civilian counterparts, she concludes.

As you read, consider the following questions:

1. According to the viewpoint, what are some of the fields in which the federal government has job openings?

2. According to Adams, what aspects of military training are considered important for federal jobs?

3. What are the requirements for a veteran to receive preference for federal jobs, according to Adams?

The federal government is hiring. With tens of thousands of jobs currently posted, in all levels of positions, and millions of employees, the federal government is the largest employer in the United States. In addition, during the next few years, over half of the current workforce will be eligible for retirement. This means there will be many openings to be filled in the future—and many opportunities to advance to more senior-level positions as the workforce retires. In addition, governmental jobs offer job security not provided by positions in the private sector.

The Federal Government Values the Experience of Veterans

Currently, the government is seeking personnel with training and experience in virtually every discipline, with an emphasis on homeland security, including security, intelligence, IT [information technology], telecommunications, logistics and health care. In addition, many of the positions require security clearance. The skills gained in the military are directly transferable to many of the positions being sought to be filled by the federal government.

In the federal government, military experience is valued. . . . With the current shortage of military personnel, some jobs previously performed by military personnel are now being performed by the civilian workforce. For these positions, along with others, including positions in the civilian military workforce, homeland security, FBI [Federal Bureau of Investigation] and CIA [Central Intelligence Agency], military skills are directly transferable. Also, certifications gained in the military—including contracting certifications and top secret clearance, are sought after by federal agencies. The training received while in the military is recognized as important for these agencies—whereas it might not be recognized as important in the private sector.

In the civilian workforce, many middle- and senior-level positions require candidates to have degrees. For the federal government, experience can often substitute for the degree. With experience in the military, a candidate without a degree can often obtain a higher level position in the federal government than in the private sector workforce.

In addition, candidates with active duty United States military service and separated under honorable conditions will likely be eligible for a veterans' preference when applying for federal jobs. This preference can help a veteran to be selected for a given position over nonveterans, as outlined below.

Veterans' Preference

Since the Civil War, veterans have been given preference in appointments to federal jobs, with Congress recognizing the sacrifices made by persons serving in the armed forces. These laws provide preference for veterans who are disabled or served in active duty during specified time periods or military campaigns over nonveterans both in hiring and in retention during reductions in force. Preference alone will not place a veteran in every federal job, nor will it apply to promotions or other in-service actions.

Generally, for a veteran to obtain preference, a veteran must have an honorable or general discharge. If a veteran retired at the rank of major/lieutenant commander or higher—and is not disabled—the veteran is not eligible for preference.

Vet Finds New Career in Department of Homeland Security

After reading about Feds Hire Vets online, I contacted several outreach specialists. . . . I received helpful résumé advice from Ms. Monica Flint. Within 30–45 days, I was scheduled for an interview with U.S. Citizenship and Immigration Services. I enjoy working for the Department of Homeland Security. I love knowing that on a daily basis I assist in securing America as well as securing America's promises to become a nation of immigrants. Meeting people from around the world and hearing their stories from life are amazing. I've had the opportunity to meet some amazing people and help change the life of families. Being a part of the Department of Homeland Security allows me to continue to serve after military life.

Bryan Boykin, "Immigration Service Analyst:
Feds Hire Vets—Vet to Vet," Feds Hire Vets, July 1, 2013.

Note that guard and reserve active duty for training does not qualify for preference. For preference to be considered, it must be indicated on the résumé.

Veterans may be eligible to have 5 points or 10 points added to their application score. If a veteran served during specific periods of conflict in the armed forces, including 1941 to 1955, 180 consecutive days from 1955 to 1976, during the Gulf War from 1990 to 1992 or in a campaign or expedition for which a campaign medal has been authorized, including El Salvador, Grenada, Haiti, Lebanon, Panama, Somalia, Southwest Asia, Bosnia and the global war on terrorism, they are eligible for a 5-point preference. For veterans who are not disabled, in addition to service, medal holders or Gulf War veterans who joined after a specific date must have served for 24 months or the full amount of time required for active duty to be eligible for the 5-point preference.

A veteran who has a service-connected disability, received a Purple Heart or is receiving compensation, disability retirement benefits or a pension from the military or the Department of Veteran Affairs may qualify for a 10-point preference. Others may claim this preference, including unmarried spouses of deceased veterans, spouses of veterans unable to work because of a service-connected disability or mothers of veterans who died in service or who are permanently and totally disabled. . . .

In addition to point preferences, there are other preferences available to veterans for federal employment. These include Veterans Recruitment Appointment (VRA), which gives federal agencies discretionary authority to hire veterans who meet the basic requirements for the position without competition. A veteran who separated from active duty in the past 3 years *and* is disabled, served on active duty during a war declared by Congress, participated while on active duty in a campaign or expedition for which a campaign badge has been authorized *or* while on active duty participated in a military operation for which the Armed Forces Service Medal was awarded is eligible for a VRA appointment. VRA authority applies to white-collar positions through the GS-11 [referring to the general schedule civil service pay scale] level.

In addition, federal agencies give noncompetitive appointments to any veteran who has a service-connected disability of 30% or more. Like the VRA, this authority is discretionary with the agency.

A veteran's status also can help in finding positions to apply for. Many job announcements in the federal government require applicants to have status—and if an applicant does not have status, they are not eligible to apply. Applicants who have served 3 years active duty in the military in the last 10 years most likely have status—according to the Veterans Employment Opportunities Act (VEOA). This is not just limited to personnel separating or retiring lower than the rank of major/lieutenant commander—it applies to all military personnel. This allows veterans to apply to positions not open to the general public—which is many of the positions posted for federal government jobs.

> "The American people and private em-
> ployers should expect that the federal
> government will be a leader by example
> in its hiring and support of veterans."

The Federal Government Does Not Hire Enough Veterans

Kent A. Eiler

Kent A. Eiler is an attorney, veteran, and captain in the US Air Force Reserve. He was counsel to the Constitution Project's Task Force on Detainee Treatment. In the following viewpoint, he argues that despite the passing of legislation such as the Veterans' Preference Act of 1944, designed to assist veterans find civilian jobs, the federal government lags behind numerous private employers in hiring veterans. Eiler points out that the interpretation of preference for veterans falls to the executive branch, which does the majority of hiring for the federal government. The executive branch has created rules, specifically applying to appointments for excepted service, that effectively nullify preference for veterans, he claims.

As you read, consider the following questions:

1. According to the viewpoint, how does the unemployment rate in 2012 for veterans of the second Gulf War compare to that of the general population?

2. How did the federal government's hiring of veterans in 2011 compare to that of DynCorp International and US Airways Group, according to Eiler?

3. What is the public's perception of post-9/11 veterans, according to the survey mentioned in the viewpoint?

The issue of veterans' unemployment is receiving considerable attention with the U.S. economy in its longest slump in decades. As U.S. involvement in the wars of Afghanistan and Iraq comes to a close, and the drawdown of service members from all branches of the U.S. military seems imminent, many observers worry veteran unemployment will increase. The reported unemployment rate for Gulf War II [also known as the Iraq War] veterans has, according to the Bureau of Labor Statistics, ping-ponged back and forth: from 8.9% in July 2012, spiking upward again to 10.9% in August 2012, and down again to 9.7% in September 2012; these statistics are well above the general population's unemployment rate that is around 8%. Politicians on all sides of the political spectrum claim to support action that will alleviate veteran unemployment and assert veterans bring invaluable skills to the civilian workforce. In this environment, one would think the federal government itself would take whatever steps it could to hire veterans. In practice, however, neither the executive branch nor the legislative branch has undertaken meaningful steps to maximize the federal government's role as a model employer. Congress has not passed significant legislation on the federal government's hiring practices since 9/11 [referring to the September 11, 2001, terrorist attacks on the United States]. Additionally, the federal government's Office of Personnel Management ("OPM") has designed rules for the government's hiring practices that effectively strip veterans of preference when they apply to a broad range of positions in the executive branch. . . .

Congressional Action on the Employment of Veterans in the Federal Government

Congress cannot compel private businesses to hire veterans; it can only encourage and cajole the private sector with incentives. At least some of the federal government's initiatives to encourage the hiring of veterans in the private sector have been praised as successful. Ultimately, the decision whether to hire a veteran rests with the individual employer in the private sector. By contrast, Congress can, and has required the federal government as an employer, to take advantage of the skill sets offered by veterans.

Though preference has been given to veterans since the Civil War, the Veterans' Preference Act of 1944 ("Veterans Act"), which incorporated prior legislation, remains the defining federal law today dealing with what government agencies must consider when filling an available vacancy. The Veterans Act identified that preference is to be given to veterans as a reward for patriotic duties by a grateful country that recognizes the sacrifices made by these veterans. Preference, as applied by the Veterans Act, includes positions in the classified civil service (now the competitive service); the unclassified civil service (positions excepted from the competitive service); the civil service of the District of Columbia; and in any temporary or emergency establishment, agency, bureau, administration, project, and department created by acts of Congress or presidential executive order. . . .

Under these rules, not every veteran is automatically eligible for preference. To qualify for preference, a veteran must have served honorably, as evidenced by nothing less than a discharge under honorable conditions. Additionally, there is a minimum amount of time he or she must have served on active duty during wartime hostilities in order to qualify. In the competitive service, the job candidate with the highest number of points will typically, though not necessarily, be awarded the vacancy. . . .

Congress has taken some positive steps in assisting veterans dealing with the pressing problem of unemployment. Specifically, it passed the Uniformed Services Employment and Reemployment Rights Act of 1994 ("USERRA") and the Veterans Employment Opportunities Act of 1998 ("VEOA") to assist veterans, reservists and members of the National Guard. Under USERRA, returning service members have to be reemployed in the job they would have retained had they not been absent because of their military service. In doing so, USERRA bolstered the reemployment rights of veterans and reservists working in the federal, state, and private sectors. . . .

Executive Branch Action on the Employment of Veterans in the Federal Government

With the action Congress has taken above, the question becomes how does the executive branch implement the law? After all, the executive branch—charged with operating the federal government with its approximately two million employees—does the bulk of hiring for the federal government. In its 1966 restructuring, Congress gave the president of the United States the ability to prescribe regulations for the admission of individuals into civil service. . . . Congress delineated civil servants into three categories: competitive service, which Congress has been very explicit in stating how veteran preference would operate; excepted service; and, later, senior executive service.

Of excepted service, Congress provided under the United States Code ("U.S.C."), 5 U.S.C. § 3320:

> The nominating or appointing authority shall select for appointment to each vacancy in the excepted service in the ex-

ecutive branch and in the government of the District of Columbia from the qualified applicants in the same manner and under the same conditions required for the competitive service by sections 5 U.S.C. 3308–3318.

Congress then delegated the responsibility for implementing § 3320 to the Office of Personnel Management ("OPM").

OPM's regulations that implement § 3320 are found in the Code of Federal Regulations ("C.F.R."), 5 C.F.R. § 302. When making an appointment in the excepted service:

> [A]n agency must make its selection from the highest available preference category, as long as at least three candidates remain in that group. When fewer than three candidates remain in the highest category, consideration may be expanded to include the next category. When making an appointment from a list on which candidates have received numerical scores, the agency must make its selection for each vacancy from not more than the highest three names available for appointment. When an agency passes over the name of a veteran entitled to priority consideration, the agency is required to record its reasons for doing so and is required to furnish a copy of those reasons to the veteran upon request.

However, OPM's regulations for the excepted service also provide "[i]n view of the circumstances and conditions surrounding employment in the following classes of positions," (i.e., positions within the excepted service which are not subject to examination or numerical evaluation), "an agency is not required to apply the appointment procedures of this part to them, but each agency shall follow the principle of veteran preference as far as administratively feasible and, on the request of a qualified and available preference eligible, shall furnish him/her with the reasons for his/her nonselection." . . .

For the exempted positions . . . OPM directed agencies to simply "follow the principle of veterans' preference as far as administratively feasible." This direction provided flexibility to federal agencies interpreting the meaning of OPM's directive. In *Patterson v. Department of the Interior*, a 2005 case before the United States Court of Appeals for the Federal Circuit, Mr. [Guy] Patterson had applied for an attorney position with the Department of the Interior. In the pleadings of the case, the Department of the Interior told the Federal Circuit it viewed Patterson's status as a veteran as a "positive factor" in its hiring decision even though he had been passed over and not offered the position. OPM viewed the "positive factor test" by the Department of the Interior as consistent with OPM's requirement that agencies "follow the principle of veteran preference as far as administratively feasible." The Federal Circuit agreed.

From a pro-veteran standpoint, the decision in the *Patterson* case highlights a huge problem with Congress's instructions for filling excepted service positions. The Federal Circuit found little of 5 U.S.C. §§ 3308–3318 relevant to filling the position that Patterson applied to in the excepted service. The Federal Circuit stated in its opinion, "Congress has not spoken on the issue of how to apply the principles of veterans' preference to positions within the excepted service that are not subject to examination." The Federal Circuit went on to say that under *Chevron, U.S.A., Inc. v. Natural Resources Defense Council, Inc.*, OPM was entitled deference in its regulations on the matter. According to the Federal Circuit, it was not the court's place to substitute the agency's interpretation of a statute with what the court thought might be better interpretation, but rather for the court to determine whether the agency's interpretation was reasonable. In this respect the Federal Circuit stated, "[T]he agency did not violate Mr. Patterson's veterans' preference rights by applying the positive factor test when it considered his application for the [attorney] position." The "positive factor test" from the *Patterson* case remains the criteria agencies and the OPM still apply today. . . .

Meaningful Action by the Federal Government to Hire Veterans

If the federal government were hiring veterans in appropriate numbers, most Americans should probably feel the current law in this area is sufficient. The problem is the federal government is doing a mediocre, if not poor, job of hiring reservists, guardsmen, and veterans; it is failing to reach the hiring numbers achieved by several private company counterparts. Gannett's *Military Times Edge* recently profiled the thirty top civilian employers of veterans, highlighting the percentage of current employees at those companies who were veterans. The federal government was not included in this profile, but a comparison of the federal government to the thirty top civilian employers of veterans illustrates the issue at the heart of this article. At a time when politicians claim to be doing all they can to alleviate veteran unemployment, the percentage of federal government employees who are veterans would not have even made *the top five* on the *Military Times Edge's* list.

In fiscal year ("FY") 2010 the Office of Personnel Management ("OPM") reported that 26.3% of the federal government's employees were veterans. The federal government hired 174,401 new employees through the first three quarters of FY 2011. Of the federal government's new hires through the first three quarters in FY 2011, 28.4% were veterans. Even though there has been an incremental rise in the federal government hiring veterans from FY 2010 to FY 2011, these percentages fall well below companies like DynCorp International Inc. and US Airways Group Inc. In FY 2011, the veterans working at DynCorp International comprised 67% of its employees, and the veterans working at US Airways comprised 35% of its employees.

While the federal government can accurately claim it is the single largest employer of veterans, with over two million employees, this cannot be the sole statistical measurement. The federal government should be a model employer that sets the standard for all other companies. The percentage of veterans the federal government employs relative to its overall workforce is a much more accurate measurement of its actual hiring support to veterans. Until this number is on par with model employers, like DynCorp and US Airways, the federal government cannot be considered the shining example it should be to pro-veteran organizations in the private sector. . . .

Revising the Federal Government's Guidelines and Changing the Culture of Misconceptions Surrounding Veterans

If the executive branch is serious about turning to veterans in its search for "highly skilled individuals to meet agency staffing needs and to support mission objectives" as the president stated, it has to deal with misconceptions that selecting authorities and hiring managers in the federal government have about veterans. The easiest way to do that is for the Office of Personnel Management ("OPM") to revise its guidelines for the hiring of veterans within the *excepted service*. Additionally, the federal government has to address the biases of its own nonveteran hiring managers.

Recently, a first-of-its-kind survey measured the general public's perceptions of post-9/11 veterans. The survey, entitled "A New Generation of Leaders," found the general public overwhelmingly regards the young men and women of the post-9/11 generation as future leaders and national assets. The survey also found that the general public believed veterans to be more disciplined, stronger in character, and more involved in their communities. Not all of the survey was positive. Negatively, the survey revealed respondents worried post-traumatic stress disorder ("PTSD") was a problem for a majority of veterans that have returned home from conflict; when in fact only about two in ten veterans will experience some level of PTSD. Additionally, the general public polled in the survey incorrectly assumed that veterans had lower levels of education and were less likely to be prepared to take a civilian job, based upon their job experience in the service, than someone who did not serve.

In *Patterson v. Department of the Interior*, Mr. Patterson's rejection letter from the Department of the Interior was included in the United States Court of Appeals for the Federal Circuit's decision. His rejection letter provides a textbook example for why so few veterans are likely in the excepted service today, and the letter reflects the negative perceptions found in the civilian survey:

> While your academic record appeared good, your résumé did not indicate any experience specifically relevant to the work of this office. Your veterans' preference was given consideration as a positive factor in the evaluation process, but as you are aware, selecting a person for an attorney position is a process that requires a careful weighing of a large number of variables. In significant part, I did not feel the preference overcame the lack of relevant experience and/or background.

The lack of background and/or relevant experience in comparison with other candidates could no doubt, or at least partially, be explained by the fact that Patterson was busy serving his country and therefore missed out on opportunities to increase his résumé as much as the other candidates. Less *relevant experience* was at least in part why the Veterans' Preference Act of 1944 ("Veterans Act") was passed; it was designed as a compensation mechanism for the fact that veterans were, invariably, older and away from civilian careers. Notwithstanding the Veterans Act, only 14.9% of employees at the Department of the Interior were veterans in FY 2011. In such an environment, one in which only a small percentage of employees are veterans, only a small percentage of employees might appreciate what a veteran's experience could bring to a particular position. In Patterson's case, he had less than a one in five chance that his job application was reviewed by a veteran.

In the *Patterson* case, Patterson's rejection letter provides a glimpse into how the positive factor test has basically rendered the Veterans Act a nullity in a huge swath of the excepted service. The rejection letter highlights that an agency's hiring process "requires a careful weighing of a large number of variables." With OPM's standard, a hiring manager in the excepted service is required to give veterans' preference no more weight than any other "positive factor" he or she might consider. . . .

The Federal Government Should Do a Better Job

The executive branch, the legislative branch, or both branches [should] simply recognize that, as a matter of fundamental fairness, a better job needs to be done to comply with the intent and spirit of the Veterans' Preference Act of 1944 ("Veterans Act"), so that the federal government serves as a model employer. We have gone from the well-intended Veterans Act in 1944 to today, when a veteran may be told her service was considered just a *positive factor* in the decision not to hire her with no real avenue of relief. The chairman of the joint chiefs [of staff], General Martin Dempsey, recently called for dialogue and "a conversation, with America" on veterans' issues, and he expressed concern about veteran unemployment. If young Americans believe they will struggle to find work after their military service concludes, fewer Americans will volunteer to serve their country in the future. A conversation is needed, and Uncle Sam needs to be able to effectively contribute to that conversation.

Veterans and the veteran organizations they belong to should understandably be patient as the federal government looks for ways to improve its hiring of veterans, but they should also expect significant, measurable progress that matches the political rhetoric. One such group, the Reserve Officers Association, at its national conventions in 2004, 2007, and 2010, passed resolutions that called for making the Veterans Act "more than an empty promise." Extolling the value of hiring veterans cannot simply be a yellow-ribbon bumper sticker for the federal government. The American people and private employers should expect that the federal government will be a leader by example in its hiring and support of veterans in the months and years ahead.

> *"The unemployment rate among veterans returning from Iraq and Afghanistan was just under 11 percent in August [2012]. It is higher for those who are younger."*

A Jobs Corps Is Needed to Put Veterans Back to Work

Bill Nelson

Bill Nelson is a Democratic US senator from Florida. In the following viewpoint, he argues that the unemployment rate for veterans of the Iraq and Afghanistan wars is high and looks to get even higher as these wars conclude. Drawing on the model of the successful Civilian Conservation Corps of the 1930s, the Veterans Jobs Corps Act has been drafted and should be passed by the Senate, Nelson contends. The senator says the act will not only reduce unemployment among veterans, but will also provide needed law enforcement and firefighters for communities as well as put human resources to work restoring and protecting public lands and waters.

Bill Nelson, "Should the Senate Pass S.3457, the Veterans Jobs Corps Act?," *Congressional Digest*, November 2012, pp. 270–272. Reproduced by permission.

As you read, consider the following questions:

1. What is the unemployment rate among Iraq and Afghanistan war veterans, according to Nelson?

2. What projects does Nelson cite as successful, smaller scale examples of a jobs corps for veterans?

3. What are some of the organizations that Nelson says support the Veterans Jobs Corps Act?

It is appropriate on this particular day, September 11—11 years ago today [September 11, 2012]—with the fact that those terrorists hijacked the four commercial airliners, causing the crashes at the World Trade Center, at the Pentagon, and in a field in Pennsylvania. What was happening also that morning was that police officers and firefighters and emergency personnel rushed to respond, and many lost their lives in attempts to save others.

The events of that morning mobilized American forces like we had not seen in years. One of the first mobilizations was our U.S. military. They were called to serve bravely in remote corners of the globe.

Veterans Face a Battle When Returning Home

Eleven years later, the mastermind of 9/11, Osama bin Laden, was taken down, we now have an al Qaeda that is severely diminished, and we are bringing our troops home from that part of the world. But for the troops, when they come home, the fight is not over. There is another fight when they get back home to America. It is a different type of battle.

The unemployment rate among veterans returning from Iraq and Afghanistan was just under 11 percent in August. It is higher for those who are younger. This problem is likely to continue to grow as we draw down in Afghanistan, as we have already drawn down in Iraq.

Support for Veterans Lacking

How does even the most dedicated Republican live with the knowledge that their party's top elected officials can so easily cast a vote to send an American solider off to war, only to refuse a comparatively small sum of money to help that veteran get his or her life back in the event they actually make it home?

Rick Ungar, "Senate GOP Obstructionists Throw Veterans Under the Bus—Vote Down Bill to Help Vets in Need of Jobs," Forbes, September 23, 2012.

It is worth noting that there have been steps made in the right direction. This past summer we passed legislation that will help veterans get federal occupational licenses when their military training matches the civilian requirements. That was a bill I had the privilege of sponsoring. It passed the Senate unanimously. It was passed by the House overwhelmingly. It was sent down, and it was signed into law. Last year, we passed the bill granting tax benefits to companies that hire wounded warriors. But we have to do more.

So we filed this legislation [the Veterans Jobs Corps Act]. . . . It is modeled after the Civilian Conservation Corps of the 1930s. The Veterans Jobs Corps would put veterans back to work restoring and protecting America's public lands and waters. The bill would also create opportunities for veterans to serve as police and firefighters and first responders.

A Track Record of Success

We have had some success on this with smaller scale projects, such as the Veterans Fire Corps pilot program at the U.S. Department of Agriculture, which trains veterans to fight forest fires. In fact, it has been so successful that folks who run these programs say they can hardly keep trainees in the program because they are picked up for full-time employment so fast. So we are expanding this idea from this pilot study that has been so successful. We are expanding it now in the Veterans Jobs Corps.

Ten percent of the money in this bill will go to hiring veterans with specialties, such as those with the specialty of military police going into civilian law enforcement and those with the specialty of medics to be firefighters and first responders.

Not only will this bill help protect our communities, but the Veterans Jobs Corps will help address the federal maintenance backlog. The National Park Service has deferred maintenance totaling over $11 billion. This backlog has been caused by the gradual shifting of funding to the operations budgets of the Park Service at the expense of everything else.

For example, at the Civil War battlefield in Fredericksburg, Virginia, a $42 million backlog in maintenance is preventing the upkeep of that vital piece of American history.

I am happy to say that a number of organizations have stepped forward to support this bill. The American Legion, the Military Officers Association of America, the Iraq and Afghanistan Veterans of America, and the National Association of Police Organizations—all of them support this legislation.

One of the greatest honors I have in this job as senator is getting out to meet and to greet current members of our military all over the globe and to thank the veterans back here at home for their service to our country.

When you meet some of these folks, both young and old, they have already done the tough, tough job, and then they come home and they have tough times as well. These folks are hardworking; they are highly trained, highly disciplined, and extremely skilled. We need to give them as many opportunities as possible to succeed when they get back home here in America.

It is up to us to stand by our soldiers, sailors, airmen, marines, and coastguardsmen.

I want to urge the Senate, when we vote today, to grant the motion for cloture so we can take up this bill and quickly pass it so those who have fought bravely for our nation can find employment when they come home.

"*Is this about veterans, or is this about politicians? I suspect it is about politicians. I suspect it is about elections and not veterans.*"

Metrics Are Needed to Determine If Existing Jobs Programs for Veterans Are Working

Tom Coburn

Tom Coburn is a Republican US senator from Oklahoma. In the following viewpoint, he argues that the Veterans Jobs Corps Act, before the US Senate in the fall of 2012, is not about helping veterans; it is a blatant and cynical attempt to use the public's support of veterans for political purposes in an election year. The senator explains that there are already six programs in place to help veterans find jobs, adding that none of these programs have any metrics attached to see if they are actually working. Coburn concludes that a better approach would be to examine the existing programs and fix them, not add another program.

Tom Coburn, "Should the Senate Pass S.3457, the Veterans Jobs Corps Act?," *Congressional Digest*, November 2012, pp. 271–277. Reproduced by permission.

As you read, consider the following questions:

1. Why does Coburn call the Veterans Jobs Corps Act discriminatory?

2. What are the six jobs programs that Coburn cites, and what does he find wrong with each of them?

3. What has happened to the national debt in the eight years that Coburn has been in the US Senate?

I come to the floor today [in November 2012] to talk about the bill that is pending [the Veterans Jobs Corps Act], and I must say: Here we go again. Let me say that what we are doing today, under the auspices of helping returning veterans get jobs—and there is nothing wrong with wanting to do that, and there is nothing wrong with trying to pay for that—is really passing a bill for political reasons so we can say we did things, because this is not going anywhere in the House of Representatives.

A couple of points I would make are that, first, yesterday, on the anniversary of 9/11 [referring to the September 11, 2001, terrorist attacks on the United States], we started the consideration of this bill, but this bill has had no hearings, no committee work, and essentially no debate until today, despite the fact that it will affect six different federal agencies, at a minimum.

Politics Motivate This Bill

The bill before the Senate provides $1 billion in mandatory spending. For the folks at home, that means it is not subject to appropriations; it will be spent, period, regardless of what we do if we pass this bill and the president signs it—over five years for the creation of a new mandatory program called the Veterans Jobs Corps.

One point I will make is that we already have six veterans' jobs programs, and not one of them has a metric on it to see if it is working. There hasn't been one hearing to see what the jobs programs we are running now are doing, to measure their effectiveness or their cost-effectiveness, and see if they are actually performing for veterans what we say we want them to do. Yet we have a bill on the floor that didn't go through that committee, where no hearings were held, and we are going to do the same thing again. Because there is not a metric in this bill.

So what is happening here is we are playing the political election card to say, how could anybody oppose a Veterans Jobs Corps bill? The real question to be asked is: How callous is it to put forth a political bill when we have no idea whether it may or may not work, for the pure political purpose of an election, without looking at the whole of the veterans' jobs programs? There is not going to be any congressional oversight on this. . . .

This legislation is going to provide $1 billion for the federal government to hire veterans on a temporary basis.

I understand that Senator [Richard] Burr's [R-NC] recommendations are going to be incorporated. That is a marked improvement to the bill. His puts them in line for a career, not a temporary job—which shows the lack of thinking because Senator Burr, the ranking member on VA [the Senate Committee on Veterans' Affairs], couldn't get a hearing. We didn't have a markup, didn't have a chance for ideas to flow through. I am not certain we are going to have amendments. I have four I would like to offer to the bill that are better pay-fors and will actually improve the bill. I am not sure we are going to do that either.

So we didn't have a hearing, and we didn't have a markup. We come to the floor, and we are not going to have amendments. What is this really all about? Is this about veterans, or is this about politicians? I suspect it is about politicians. I suspect it is about elections and not veterans.

This Bill Discriminates Against Some Veterans

The legislation grants broad authority to the Department of Justice, Department of Defense, Department of Labor, Department of Agriculture, Department of Commerce, Department of Homeland Security, the Interior Department, and the Army Corps of Engineers to hire veterans in jobs such as conservation and first responders.

However, to comply with the pay-go rules, we manipulate the system again. We include revenue increases to equal the cost of the bill. We do that by requiring a continuous levy on payments to Medicare providers and suppliers—which is not a bad idea—and also by denying or revoking passports in cases of seriously delinquent taxes. I have heard that is going to be pulled, but nobody knows. Nobody has seen it. That is why we have committees, so we don't have to play with things before we have a base bill and we know what it will do.

The bill already violates the Budget Control Act's allocation for [Department of] Veterans Affairs funding. It is subject to a 302(f) [of the act, prohibiting consideration of legislation that exceeds certain allocations] point of order because it is outside the bounds of their appropriations.

The bill also states a distinct preference for veterans of the current war in Afghanistan and the most recent war in Iraq by stating that these jobs are primarily for veterans who have served since September 11, 2001.

As with the veterans' caregiver bill in 2009, this is blatant discrimination against our other veterans. One class of veterans is better than another class of veterans? Tell me how. Is somebody who died in the Vietnam War less honorable than somebody who has given their life in Afghanistan? Yet we are making that distinction in terms of the benefits available to those who served our country honorably.

So we are blatantly discriminating against veterans who served before 9/11. I would also remind us that those veterans didn't have the Post-9/11 GI Bill [Post-9/11 Veterans Educational Assistance Act]. They didn't have the other significant benefits that have come along and been passed down, both paid benefits, family transfer of the post-9/11 bill, or the educational benefits for in-service that the present veterans have.

Many Programs for Veterans Already Exist

Another thing I would remind my colleagues is that right now there is a preference in every branch of the federal government for hiring veterans. It is already written into law. Since 1944, the federal government has stated that veterans with honorable or general discharges are preferred for hiring in competitive positions and may also be hired without competition in many cases. In other words, they get an absolute preference. Disabled veterans get even a higher preference over nondisabled veterans. Veterans also have priority in retention in terms of government downsizing: If you were a veteran, you don't get downsized; if you are not a veteran, you will.

Senator Burr's bill—which it appears the majority will take and add to their bill rather than replace their bill—will direct the Office of Personnel Management to require that each of the 10,000 job vacancies presently in the federal government today should be filled by veterans. This would actually provide a real career path for veterans, not a temporary make-work job slot that will go away as soon as the $1 billion runs out.

According to a 2011 GAO [Government Accountability Office] report, there are six job training programs, which I have outlined, already on the books. They are not working, but they are on the books, and we are spending money on them. We have no metrics to know whether they are working. We have had no oversight hearings to know whether they are working. None has ever been held.

There is the Labor Department's Disabled Veterans' Outreach Program. It does job readiness, skills training, retention training, and employment counseling. The Labor Department's Homeless Veterans' Reintegration Project does everything the first one I mentioned does. The Labor Department's [Local] Veterans' Employment Representative Program does exactly the same thing as the first two. The Labor Department's Transition Assistance Program does job search and job readiness training. The Labor Department's Veterans Workforce Investment [Program], again, does all the same tasks as the first two I mentioned.

The [Department of] Veterans Affairs' rehabilitation for disabled veterans program does nearly everything from job training to employment counseling to job referral to on-the-job training to basic adult literacy.

This bill and those training programs are in addition to the Post-9/11 GI Bill and the tuition assistance program, which provides 100 percent tuition assistance plus expenses, plus a monthly stipend salary for unemployed or any other veterans to attend college, vocational training, pursue licensure, with fees paid for by the federal government, and allows them to transfer this benefit to their spouses.

No One Knows If Existing Programs Work

The question I have, with that benefit—and we are doing another one now for political purposes, not because we really care about veterans—[is] why isn't this one working? We are going to spend billions on the Post-9/11 GI Bill, and we are going to pay them at the rate of a noncommissioned officer all the time they are going to college. Why isn't that working? Where is the oversight hearing to see why what we just did two years ago isn't working?

Instead, what we are going to do is—which the Congress has done under both Democrats and Republicans—we are going to throw in more money and do another one. Instead of

Media Faults GOP on Jobs Bill

The narrative regarding this bill seems to have cast the GOP [Republican Party] in the role of villains and with Democrats claiming nobility and benevolence, consistent with oft-seen stereotypes. In actuality, the supposed core philosophies both have some merit—the Democrats giving more credence to taxation and the government itself being put to good use helping people, in contrast to the GOP preference that government should be limited, especially when there is so much debt.

Craig Berlin,
"Reinforcing Preconceived Notions Again:
Veterans Jobs Bill Details Elude Media,"
Examiner.com, September 23, 2012.

measuring what works and measuring what we are doing, we are going to create another program. Granted, supposedly it is only five years.

When it comes to five years, what will happen whether it works or not? Nobody will vote against extending the veterans program, will they? How can anyone be against veterans?

So we would not do the hard work of having committee hearings; we would not do the oversight. We would not even change this bill to make sure it has absolute metrics on what it is doing. So we are continuing down the road to bankruptcy, all in the name of putting a bill—that isn't going to pass the House—on the Senate floor so two or three members or the Senate can go home and claim they did something.

I think it is hypocritical. Those 13 Oklahomans who died in Afghanistan this last year from the Oklahoma National Guard . . . represented the real value of America. This bill doesn't.

The Post-9/11 GI Bill pays 100 percent of the highest cost public school in any state. So veterans can go to the best public school paid for completely by the government if they are a post-9/11 veteran. They can get the same equivalent pay as a noncommissioned officer the time they are going. That is what we have already got out there.

Without this legislation, today any unemployed veteran who can get into a community college can go for free, receive three years of pay, all their expenses paid, their housing paid—all of those things paid.

Well, if that isn't working, why isn't it working? Where is the hearing to find out why that isn't working? No, we are just going to pass another bill without a hearing, without a committee markup, for politically expedient purposes. Oh, it is just $1 billion.

Where is our honor? Where is our valor? Where is our sacrifice?

The Department of Defense tuition assistance program, another program, while you are in the military, is paid for. All you have to do is make a C or better—online, off-line, whatever way you want to go.

So let me summarize: We have the tuition assistance program, we have the Post-9/11 GI Bill, we have the GI Bill, we have six separate VA job programs. We have a bill on the floor to do another one, and nobody is asking the questions what is wrong with what we are doing now, and why aren't we fixing it?

This Bill Would Contribute to the National Debt

If what we are doing now isn't working, why aren't we fixing that? Why aren't we going to allow amendments to fix things? Why are we going to fill the tree and not allow the process that our founders designed for the Senate to work so that all ideas could be considered?

No, this is a political exercise. I am going to call it what it is. This isn't about veterans; this is about politicians. My hope is that we wake up before our country fails.

When I came to the Senate, the average family's responsibility for public debt per individual was $26,000. Within the 8 years I have been here, it is now 51,400 and some odd dollars. We are playing a game. We are thinking short term. We are worried about political careers and elections, but we are not worried about the country. This is about the greatest example of the incompetence of the Congress of the United States I have ever seen.

I am for helping veterans, I am for paying for it, and I am for making sure they get rewarded for their service and their sacrifice. This bill isn't it. This is a charade. That is exactly what it is. To call it anything else dishonors the service of those who have defended and protected our country.

| "Hiring a veteran can be one of the best
business decisions you make."

More Employers Are Finding That Veterans Make Good Employees

Carl M. Cannon

Carl M. Cannon is the Washington bureau chief for RealClear-Politics. In the following viewpoint, Cannon argues that concerns about unemployment and underemployment among war veterans is not a new problem, stating that it can be traced back to the American Civil War. The United States has gradually introduced programs to help returning veterans, most notably the GI Bill, he states. At the present time, there are numerous initiatives sponsored by both public and private sectors in support of hiring veterans. Many businesses support these initiatives because veterans possess leadership skills, character, and discipline that make them good employees, he concludes.

As you read, consider the following questions:

1. According to the Center for a New American Security report, what are some of the concerns that employers have in hiring veterans?

2. What are some of the public and private sector initiatives supporting the hiring of veterans that the author cites?

3. According to Steve Toomey, why do veterans make good railroad employees?

Confiding to a friend after her son returned from the Civil War, a Massachusetts mother named Henrietta Maria Benson Homer wrote: "He came home so changed that his best friends did not know him, but is well & all right now."

Civil War Veterans Feared Unemployment

One factor in helping make her son "well" is that he started working again. Painting would become his trade—the young man's name was Winslow Homer—and in those days Americans awaited the work of master painters the way we anticipate the latest release from moviemakers such as Steven Spielberg or Kathryn Bigelow.

In the autumn of 1865, Winslow Homer unveiled a work titled *The Veteran in a New Field*, depicting a returning Union soldier harvesting an abundant crop of wheat. At first glance, it is a hopeful image intended to comfort a nation wracked by the carnage of war and martyrdom of Abraham Lincoln.

But contemporary Americans who gazed at that painting closely noticed a couple of disquieting details. For one thing, there was that title. The field Winslow Homer painted is not "new." It's a mature one, ripe for the reaping in late summer, when the image was being painted. That title refers to both the man's "new" profession—farming, not soldiering—

with its reminder that some of the bloodiest fighting in the Civil War took place in wheat fields.

Some viewers who looked even closer noticed something else. The single-bladed scythe in the painting is a familiar image: It's that of the Grim Reaper, another reference to the killing fields of the Civil War. But that's not all it meant.

That type of scythe was out of date by 1865. The point here is that the soldier's skills—and his tools—had also become obsolete while he was away at the front. Homer was touching on a recurring fear of those in uniform: Even if they make it through alive—even if they make it through unscathed—will there still be a place for them in their nation's workforce?

A Mixed Record on Hiring Veterans

It's a worry men shared at Shiloh and Cold Harbor. They thought of home—and of what work might await them—in the trenches at Belleau Wood, the rain forests of the Solomon Islands, the beaches of Sicily, the snows of North Korea, the jungles of Vietnam, the deserts of Mesopotamia, and the arid moonscape of Kandahar.

Some share it even after they return home. "I'm scared," one recently mustered young soldier from Augusta, Ga., told a private sector recruiter. "I don't know what to do."

Gradually, this country that sends these warriors abroad has learned what do to. It was a lesson forged painfully, and in fits and starts.

In 1924, Congress passed a law guaranteeing bonus payments to the veterans of the American Expeditionary Forces—the "doughboys" who marched in 1917 with Gen. John J. Pershing into the "war to end all wars." The catch was that the money wasn't to be paid until 1945. In the Roaring Twenties, this was acceptable. But when the 1930s ushered in a severe economic depression that left most of the veterans out of work, they marched on Washington.

This "Bonus Expeditionary Force" camped in the nation's capital. The House of Representatives voted to pay them immediately, but the Senate refused. The Bonus Army decided to remain in Washington—until they were rousted on President [Herbert] Hoover's orders by U.S. Army regulars under the command of Gen. Douglas MacArthur and led in the field by a junior officer named George Patton.

As the flames of the veterans' temporary homes lit up Washington's nighttime sky, one MacArthur military aide was stricken. His name was Dwight Eisenhower, and by the time the millions of troops under his command were mustered out of service at the end of World War II, their return to civilian life would be eased by the GI Bill [Servicemen's Readjustment Act of 1944].

But the nation's appreciation for its military veterans is not a straight line. Returning Vietnam veterans were advised not to show up for job interviews in their uniforms, even if they were still in the service. They were called names by strangers, and asked offensive questions by prospective employers.

Today we are doing better. Veterans are applauded at every home baseball game in Washington, D.C., and serenaded at public events around the country. It's not uncommon today to see a well-heeled traveler give up his seat in first class to a uniformed member of the military heading overseas—or home for a well-deserved break.

Such gestures are appreciated, but what those veterans want from society even more when they arrive home for good is the same as ever: They want the chance to apply their skills and training to a job in the civilian sector. Here, the nation's record is mixed.

Why We Hire

The U.S. military presence in Iraq and Afghanistan has now lasted a dozen years. For the last 4½ years, veterans leaving the service have found themselves attempting to assimilate into an economy in which the official unemployment rate has been around 8 percent, with the real number significantly higher.

Veterans have not been immune from these macroeconomic problems—and veterans in the 18–24 age range have fared even worse.

"This does not make any sense," President [Barack] Obama said on April 30 [2013]. "If you can save a life on the battlefield, then you sure as heck can save one in an ambulance in a state-of-the-art hospital. If you can oversee a convoy of equipment and track millions of dollars of assets, then you can run a company's supply chain or you can balance its books. If you can lead a platoon in a war zone, then I think you can lead a team in a conference center."

A 2012 report by the nonpartisan Center for a New American Security details some of employers' concerns. They range from difficulties translating veterans' skills to those of their industries to worries about accommodating veterans with injuries, including the psychic wounds of post-traumatic stress disorder. Many employers also conceded that in this era of seemingly unending wars, they worry about future deployments by the newly hired veterans, many of whom remain in the National Guard or the reserves.

Yet the detailed interviews with nearly 90 employers turned up many more reasons for putting ex-military employees on the payroll. "Hiring veterans is good business," the report concluded. "The companies reported 11 reasons they hire veterans, with an emphasis on veterans' leadership and teamwork skills, character and discipline."

This conclusion is becoming a consensus, in both the public and private sectors, and in polarized Washington it is one of those rare issues on which there seems to be little daylight between liberals and conservatives.

A Mandate to Hire Veterans

The Veterans Opportunity to Work Act of 2011, which grants tax credits to employers who hire veterans, passed the Republican-controlled House by 418–6 and the Democratic-controlled Senate, 95–0. It was embraced by President Obama, who signed it on Nov. 21, 2011, with a ringing call to action.

"Today, because Democrats and Republicans came together, I'm proud to sign those proposals into law—and I urge every business owner out there who's hiring to hire a vet right away," the commander in chief said. "Today the message is simple: For businesses out there, if you are hiring, hire a veteran. It's the right thing to do for you, it's the right thing to do for them, and it's the right thing to do for our economy."

The administration has retained this focus. Even before the law had passed, the president challenged U.S. employers to hire 100,000 veterans by 2013. First Lady Michelle Obama and vice-presidential spouse Jill Biden launched an initiative called Joining Forces to keep a focus on this topic and other issues pertaining to veterans and their families.

Mrs. Obama and Mrs. Biden noted two weeks ago at a White House event that the nation's employers had tripled their 100,000-vet goal, and had done so eight months early. "Today is simply just a mile marker, and we're not going to stop until every single veteran or military spouse that is searching for a job has found one," the first lady said while looking directly at the military families assembled in the room. "We will stand with you now and for decades to come."

In this cause, the administration was not starting an effort; it was adding the prestige of the White House to an effort already well under way. In March of 2011, the U.S. Chamber of Commerce—the president's nemesis on many issues—began hosting job fairs around the country as part of its "Hiring Our Heroes" initiative. The Chamber has now sponsored some 400 such job fairs.

Hiring Veterans Makes Good Business Sense

Meanwhile, individual companies—and entire industry sectors—have stepped up. McDonald's promised to hire 100,000 veterans itself over the next three years. Walmart CEO [chief executive officer] Bill Simon followed that announcement by vowing that, beginning on Memorial Day, the retail giant will offer a job to any man or woman honorably discharged by this country's armed forces.

"Hiring a veteran can be one of the best business decisions you make," he said. "Veterans have a record of performance under pressure."

In making such assertions, executives are deferring to veterans' sensibilities, as well as a fiduciary responsibility to their own shareholders. The main reason for hiring veterans, they say, is that it's good for business.

"Veterans are a good match for the railroads," says Steve Toomey, manager of military and diversity recruiting for the CSX Corp. "Veterans have an appreciation of safety procedures and logistics, many have been trained in leadership, and they have demonstrated a willingness to relocate."

So it makes sense that in *G.I. Jobs* magazine's annual ranking of veteran-friendly employers, the railroad industry is well represented every year. (In 2013, all four major railroads were among the top 30, and two of them—CSX and Burlington Northern and Santa Fe—were among the top five, along with USAA [United Services Automobile Association], Booz Allen Hamilton, and Deloitte.)

But it's not the only reason. "We also see hiring veterans to be one of our social responsibilities as a corporation," Toomey said in an interview.

In other words, although Mitt Romney might have been tone deaf when he told a heckler, "Corporations are people, my friend," he wasn't wrong. . . .

That young combat veteran in Augusta, Ga., who admitted that he found the process of looking for work quite daunting, was confiding his fears to Steve Toomey. The CSX recruiter calmed him down with some simple advice. "That's okay," he told the young man soothingly. "Let's make a plan."

Periodical and Internet Sources Bibliography

The following articles have been selected to supplement the diverse views presented in this chapter.

Michael Cooney	"White House Wants 5,000 Veterans in Wireless Tech Jobs by 2015," *Network World*, November 20, 2013.
Anne Field	"Veterans Find Jobs Program Works: New Skills and Group Placement Help 13 Vets Overcome Long Odds of Finding a Job," *Crain's New York Business*, September 22, 2013.
Mary Flynn	"Young Veterans Face Soaring Unemployment Levels; Employers Find Ways to Skirt USERRA Laws," *The Officer*, November–December 2013.
Fawn Johnson	"Paying Veterans to Give Back," *National Journal*, January 14, 2014.
James J. Jones and Dan Goldenberg	"Pentagon Partly to Blame for High Veteran Unemployment Rate?," FoxNews.com, March 22, 2014.
Karen Nozik	"Mission Outdoors: Sierra Club Program Provides Healing and Camaraderie for War Veterans," *National Parks*, Summer 2013.
Michelle Obama and Jill Biden	"Businesses Must Hire More Vets," *Fortune*, April 30, 2013.
Emmet Pierce	"Veterans May Face Private Sector Obstacle Course in Job Search," *San Diego Business Journal*, July 22, 2013.
Brad Plumer	"The Unemployment Rate for Recent Veterans Is Incredibly High," *Washington Post*, November 11, 2013.
Kelly Wallace	"Why Do So Many Female Veterans Struggle to Find Work?," CNN, November 13, 2014.

How Can Suicide Among Veterans Be Prevented?

Chapter Preface

Every day, twenty-two veterans commit suicide in the United States, according to a study released in February 2012 by the Department of Veterans Affairs (VA). The study was based on data collected from twenty-one states from 1999 to 2011. This grim statistic prompted talk of a veteran suicide epidemic and served as a call to action for veterans' advocacy groups. Paul Rieckhoff, founder and chief executive officer of the Iraq and Afghanistan Veterans of America, called suicide prevention the number one priority of his group. "The suicide rate is out of control. We're losing roughly 22 veterans per day to suicide. . . . We are losing more people now to suicide than to combat," he said in a November 2013 article at CNN.com.

Unveiling his administration's health and education initiatives to a group of disabled veterans in Florida in August 2013, President Barack Obama cited $107 million in new funding for mental health treatment, saying, "we have to end this epidemic of suicides among our veterans and troops."

According to CNN reporter Moni Basu, the number of veteran suicides is probably even higher than reported. Part of the problem is that it is up to the funeral director or coroner to enter veteran status and cause of death on the death certificate. Sometimes, veteran status is unknown to the funeral director or coroner, and some deaths—such as deliberate car accidents and drug overdoses—may not be listed as suicides.

Whether or not there is a suicide epidemic among veterans is a matter for debate. The Department of Veterans Affairs discounts claims of an epidemic, pointing to statistics that show that the number of suicides overall in the United States increased by approximately 11 percent between 2007 and 2010. "There is a perception that we have a veterans' suicide epidemic on our hands. I don't think that is true," said Robert

Bossarte, an epidemiologist with the VA who conducted the study. "The rate is going up in the country, and veterans are a part of it."

Forbes contributor Tim Worstall sides with the VA, saying "Is the number of military suicides growing? It would appear so, but then so is the number of veterans, so that isn't entirely a surprise. But if the actual rate of suicide among current and past military members is the same (or possibly even a little lower) than that in the general population, then it's very difficult indeed to conclude that we [have] an 'epidemic' going on."

As the veteran population grows, some fear that suicides among veterans will become an even more significant issue. In the following chapter, commentators offer differing opinions on the causes of and solutions for veteran suicide.

"*We've decreased the suicide rate among younger veterans, those 18 to 29 years old, who use VA health care services.*"

The Department of Veterans Affairs Is Making Progress in Suicide Prevention

Cheryl Pellerin

Cheryl Pellerin is a reporter and science writer at the American Forces Press Service. In the following viewpoint, she points out that Dr. Robert Petzel, the Department of Veterans Affairs (VA) undersecretary for health at the time, reported that the additional staff and programs that the VA has added have been effective in reducing suicide rates among younger veterans. She further reports that the VA is making improvements in treating such conditions as substance abuse and depression, which are linked to suicide among veterans.

As you read, consider the following questions:

1. According to Pellerin, how has the use of the VA for mental health care increased since 2007?

Cheryl Pellerin, "VA Boosts Staffing, Programs to Prevent Suicide," American Forces Press Service, June 22, 2012. Reproduced by permission.

2. How many mental health professionals does the VA employ, and how many more is it hiring, according to the viewpoint?

3. What does Pellerin say is the therapy that the VA uses to treat post-traumatic stress disorder?

The Department of Veterans Affairs (VA) is making progress in suicide prevention, adding staff and programs to treat the "invisible scars" carried home from the war by service members and veterans, the VA undersecretary for health said this week [in June 2012].

More Veterans Seek Mental Health Treatment at VA

Speaking at the June 20–22 Annual DoD/VA Suicide Prevention Conference here, Dr. Robert Petzel addressed hundreds of mental health professionals, clinicians, military leaders and family members.

"America's veterans particularly deserve the best care this nation and our departments can offer them, as do America's service members," Petzel said.

He said metrics for progress at the VA include, for example, a constant suicide rate they use for middle-aged male veterans as rates for the same age group in the general population rise.

And "we've decreased the suicide rate among younger veterans, those 18 to 29 years old, who use VA health care services," Petzel said, noting suicide rates are lower among veterans in general who receive mental health treatment at the VA.

More veterans than ever turn to the VA for help, Petzel said, adding that the organization has seen a 35 percent increase since 2007 in the number of veterans who receive mental health care.

Today the VA spends $6.2 billion a year on care for about 1.5 million veterans, he said.

Knowing Risk Factors Can Prevent Suicide

The likelihood of suicide can be reduced with timely intervention. Research suggests that the best way to prevent suicide is to know the risk factors, be alert to the signs of depression and other mental disorders, recognize the warning signs, and intervene before the person can complete the process of self-destruction.

Mark R. Lis,
"Be a Good Wingman: Know the Signals
That Someone Might Be Contemplating Suicide,"
Citizen Airman, *August 2013.*

"To meet this increased need and demand, [VA secretary Eric] Shinseki has increased the number of programs, people and resources that we're devoting to veterans' mental health services," Petzel explained.

The VA employs 21,000 mental health professionals, and in the last four weeks VA officials announced that it is hiring another 1,900 mental health providers.

"Within six months," Petzel said, "we expect to have on board approximately 23,000 clinical psychologists, psychiatrists, psychiatric social workers, psychiatric mental health nurses and clinical counselors."

The VA is also making progress in addressing some of the troubling mental health problems that many veterans face and that are correlated with suicide, he added.

"For the past decade we've made significant improvements in substance-use-disorder treatment using evidence-based psychotherapies for problems like depression and providing mental health care in our primary care . . . clinics," he said.

VA Has Developed a New PTSD Therapy

The VA also developed a therapy for post-traumatic stress disorder [PTSD] that has been shown to work in clinical trials.

The therapy treats "PTSD by repeatedly exposing veterans to the triggers that make them anxious," Petzel said. "These prolonged exposures help veterans get used to their bad memories so that they can eventually be free of the debilitating consequences of those memories."

During his presentation, Petzel announced that the VA is launching a new program to help veterans with PTSD. The AboutFace campaign, he said, features personal videos of veterans from all eras who have experienced PTSD and turned their lives around with treatment.

"Through the videos, viewers meet veterans and hear how PTSD affected them and their loved ones," Petzel said. "But most importantly, visitors to this website can also learn the steps to gain control over their lives."

AboutFace was designed as a complementary campaign to VA's Make the Connection campaign, which uses personal testimonials to illustrate true stories of veterans who faced experiences, physical ailments or psychological symptoms, and reached out for help and found ways to overcome their challenges.

Petzel also announced that the VA has set a goal to conduct more than 200,000 clinically based teleconferenced mental health consultations in 2012.

This follows the decision last month to stop charging veterans a co-payment when they receive mental health care at home, he said.

"VA health care professionals do this by using video teleconferencing, connecting with patients or connecting with patients and a consulting physician," he explained.

The VA is reaching more veterans through tele–mental health and mobile technologies, the undersecretary said, adding, "I believe that VA is the largest user of tele–mental health and the largest user of tele-health across the country."

Despite progress in many areas, Petzel said, the VA recognizes "that we cannot meet this challenge alone. To ensure that service members, veterans and their families get the care they need and deserve, we all must collaborate and we must collaborate with the community."

All mental health and substance abuse health care providers across the government, communities and the private sector "must partner and all must share responsibility for zero tolerance for suicide," Petzel said.

> "We enlist soldiers to protect us, but when they come home we don't protect them."

A Veteran's Death, the Nation's Shame

Nicholas D. Kristof

Nicholas D. Kristof is a Pulitzer Prize–winning columnist for the New York Times. In the following viewpoint, he argues that there have been more veteran suicides per year than the number of soldiers killed in battle in Iraq and Afghanistan since those wars began. He speculates that a contributing factor to this alarming suicide rate is the high incidence of post-traumatic stress disorder and traumatic brain injury. Although the Department of Veterans Affairs is making efforts to prevent suicides among veterans, it is not doing nearly enough, Kristof maintains.

As you read, consider the following questions:

1. What percentage of veterans from the Afghanistan and Iraq wars are affected by post-traumatic stress disorder or traumatic brain injury, according to the study cited by Kristof?

2. How does the fact of being a veteran age seventeen to twenty-four impact the risk of suicide, according to a study in the *American Journal of Public Health*?

3. How many new veterans will there be in the next five years, according to the viewpoint?

Here's a window into a tragedy within the American military: For every soldier killed on the battlefield this year [2012], about 25 veterans are dying by their own hands.

An American soldier dies every day and a half, on average, in Iraq or Afghanistan. Veterans kill themselves at a rate of one every 80 minutes. More than 6,500 veteran suicides are logged every year—more than the total number of soldiers killed in Afghanistan and Iraq combined since those wars began.

Mental Health Issues Linked to Suicide

These unnoticed killing fields are places like New Middletown, Ohio, where Cheryl DeBow raised two sons, Michael and Ryan Yurchison, and saw them depart for Iraq. Michael, then 22, signed up soon after the 9/11 attacks [referring to the September 11, 2001, terrorist attacks on the United States].

"I can't just sit back and do nothing," he told his mom. Two years later, Ryan followed his beloved older brother to the army.

When Michael was discharged, DeBow picked him up at the airport—and was staggered. "When he got off the plane and I picked him up, it was like he was an empty shell," she told me. "His body was shaking." Michael began drinking and abusing drugs, his mother says, and he terrified her by buying the same kind of gun he had carried in Iraq. "He said he slept with his gun over there, and he needed it here," she recalls.

Then Ryan returned home in 2007, and he too began to show signs of severe strain. He couldn't sleep, abused drugs and alcohol, and suffered extreme jitters.

"He was so anxious, he couldn't stand to sit next to you and hear you breathe," DeBow remembers. A talented film-maker, Ryan turned the lens on himself to record heartbreaking video of his own sleeplessness, his own irrational behavior—even his own mock suicide.

One reason for veteran suicides (and crimes, which get far more attention) may be post-traumatic stress disorder, along with a related condition, traumatic brain injury. Ryan suffered a concussion in an explosion in Iraq, and Michael finally had traumatic brain injury diagnosed two months ago [February 2012].

Estimates of post-traumatic stress disorder and traumatic brain injury vary widely, but a ballpark figure is that the problems afflict at least one in five veterans from Afghanistan and Iraq. One study found that by their third or fourth tours in Iraq or Afghanistan, more than one-quarter of soldiers had such mental health problems.

Preliminary figures suggest that being a veteran now roughly doubles one's risk of suicide. For young men ages 17 to 24, being a veteran almost quadruples the risk of suicide, according to a study in the *American Journal of Public Health*.

Department of Veterans Affairs Does Not Do Enough

Michael and Ryan, like so many other veterans, sought help from the Department of Veterans Affairs [VA]. Eric Shinseki, the secretary of veterans affairs, declined to speak to me, but the most common view among those I interviewed was that the VA has improved but still doesn't do nearly enough about the suicide problem.

"It's an epidemic that is not being addressed fully," said Bob Filner, a Democratic congressman from San Diego and the senior Democrat on the House Veterans' Affairs Committee. "We could be doing so much more."

To its credit, the VA has established a suicide hotline and appointed suicide-prevention coordinators. It is also chipping away at a warrior culture in which mental health concerns are considered sissy. Still, veterans routinely slip through the cracks. Last year, the United States Court of Appeals in San Francisco excoriated the VA for "unchecked incompetence" in dealing with veterans' mental health.

Patrick Bellon, head of Veterans for Common Sense, which filed the suit in that case, says the VA has genuinely improved but is still struggling. "There are going to be one million new veterans in the next five years," he said. "They're already having trouble coping with the population they have now, so I don't know what they're going to do."

Last month, the VA's own inspector general reported on a 26-year-old veteran who was found wandering naked through traffic in California. The police tried to get care for him, but a VA hospital reportedly said it couldn't accept him until morning. The young man didn't go in, and after a series of other missed opportunities to get treatment, he stepped in front of a train and killed himself.

A Delay in Treatment Led to a Suicide

Likewise, neither Michael nor Ryan received much help from VA hospitals. In early 2010, Ryan began to talk more about suicide, and DeBow rushed him to emergency rooms and pleaded with the VA for help. She says she was told that an inpatient treatment program had a six-month waiting list. (The VA says it has no record of a request for hospitalization for Ryan.)

Court Blasts VA for Mental Health Failures

There comes a time when the political branches have so completely and chronically failed to respect the people's constitutional rights that the courts must be willing to enforce them. We have reached that unfortunate point with respect to veterans who are suffering from the hidden, or not hidden, wounds of war. The VA's [Department of Veterans Affairs'] unchecked incompetence has gone on long enough; no more veterans should be compelled to agonize or perish while the government fails to perform its obligations. Having chosen to honor and provide for our veterans by guaranteeing them the mental health care and other critical benefits to which they are entitled, the government may not deprive them of that support through unchallengeable and interminable delays. Because the VA continues to deny veterans what they have been promised without affording them the process due to them under the Constitution, our duty is to compel the agency to provide the procedural safeguards that will ensure their rights.

Stephen Reinhardt, Opinion,
Veterans for Common Sense v. Eric K. Shinseki,
United States Court of Appeals for the Ninth Circuit,
May 10, 2011.

"Ryan was hurting, saying he was going to end it all, stuff like that," recalls his best friend, Steve Schaeffer, who served with him in Iraq and says he has likewise struggled with the VA to get mental health services. "Getting an appointment is like pulling teeth," he said. "You get an appointment in six weeks when you need it today."

While Ryan was waiting for a spot in the addiction program, in May 2010, he died of a drug overdose. It was listed as an accidental death, but family and friends are convinced it was suicide.

The heartbreak of Ryan's death added to his brother's despair, but DeBow says Michael is now making slow progress. "He is able to get out of bed most mornings," she told me. "That is a huge improvement." Michael asked not to be interviewed: He wants to look forward, not back.

As for DeBow, every day is a struggle. She sent two strong, healthy men to serve her country, and now her family has been hollowed in ways that aren't as tidy, as honored, or as easy to explain as when the battle wounds are physical. I wanted to make sure that her family would be comfortable with the spotlight this article would bring, so I asked her why she was speaking out.

"When Ryan joined the army, he was willing to sacrifice his life for his country," she said. "And he did, just in a different way, without the glory. He would want it this way."

"My home has been a nightmare," DeBow added through tears, recounting how three of Ryan's friends in the military have killed themselves since their return. "You hear my story, but it's happening everywhere."

We refurbish tanks after time in combat, but don't much help men and women exorcise the demons of war. Presidents commit troops to distant battlefields, but don't commit enough dollars to veterans' services afterward. We enlist soldiers to protect us, but when they come home we don't protect them.

"Things need to change," DeBow said, and her voice broke as she added: "These are guys who went through so much. If anybody deserves help, it's them."

> *"The number of military and veteran suicides is rising, and experts fear it will continue to rise despite aggressive suicide prevention campaigns by the government and private organizations."*

Military and Veteran Suicides Rise Despite Aggressive Prevention Efforts

David Wood

David Wood is the senior military correspondent for the Huffington Post. *His series on wounded veterans of Iraq and Afghanistan won the 2012 Pulitzer Prize for national reporting. In the following viewpoint, Wood argues that post-9/11 veterans have been subjected to a number of stressful experiences that are linked to suicide. He adds that these stresses are responsible for an increase in active-duty military and veteran suicides. Although the Pentagon and Department of Veterans Affairs have developed a number of mental health programs designed to prevent suicides, more needs to be done, Wood maintains, particularly to identify those at risk and to intervene at an early stage.*

As you read, consider the following questions:

1. What statistic does Wood cite to support his contention that mental stress within the military is high?

2. What is "adjustment reaction," according to Wood?

3. According to the viewpoint, what are some of the reasons why veterans under stress don't seek help?

The good news: Most people with military service never consider suicide. Contrary to popular perception, there is no "epidemic" of military-related suicides—even though President Barack Obama used the word in a speech this summer [2013] at the Disabled American Veterans [National] Convention. Among those few whose lives do spiral down toward darkness and despair, the vast majority never take that irrevocable step.

Demographics Suggest an Increase in Veteran Suicides

The bad news: The number of military and veteran suicides is rising, and experts fear it will continue to rise despite aggressive suicide prevention campaigns by the government and private organizations.

The Pentagon and Department of Veterans Affairs (VA), already struggling to meet an increasing demand from troops and veterans for mental health services, are watching the suicide rates, and the growing number of those considered "at risk" of suicide, with apprehension.

"It really is extremely concerning," said Caitlin Thompson, a VA psychologist and clinical care coordinator at the national crisis line for the military and veterans.

The warning signs of an approaching wave of suicides are unmistakable.

- While the rate of suicides has traditionally been lower for the military ranks than for civilians, that trend has begun to reverse.

- The number of suicides among active-duty troops of all services remains relatively low, at 350 last year, Pentagon data show. But that number has more than doubled since 2001, while in the army's active-duty ranks, suicides have tripled during the same period, from 52 soldiers in 2001 to 185 last year.

- Roughly half of active-duty troops who die by suicide never served in Iraq or Afghanistan. But there is growing evidence that war trauma weighs heavily on those who did. In one indication of deep emotional stress, the suicide rate among U.S. troops deployed to Iraq between 2004 and 2007, a period of intensified fighting, jumped from 13.5 to 24.8 per 100,000, according to a report issued in 2009 by the army surgeon general.

- Some 8,000 veterans are thought to die by suicide each year, a toll of about 22 per day, according to a 2012 VA study. The VA acknowledged the numbers might be significantly underestimated because they're based on incomplete data from 21 states, not including Texas or California. Even so, the data documents an increase of nearly 11 percent between 2007 and 2010, the most recent year of data in the study.

- The population of veterans over 50—more than two-thirds of all veterans—is swelling with aging baby boomers. Mostly men, they are considered more at risk of suicide because they tend to be socially isolated, struggle with physical or mental deterioration, and possess easy familiarity with firearms.

The suicide numbers are rising despite a determined push by the Pentagon and the VA to connect troops to a proliferation of resources. These range from immediate crisis intervention, to specific therapy for post-traumatic stress disorder and other forms of trauma, to broader mental health services, peer mentoring, resiliency training, and financial and relationship counseling. VA specialists scour hundreds of places, from NASCAR events to American Indian reservations, for veterans in need. There is such a drive to provide resources that even the Pentagon can't say how many programs it has or what they cost.

Suicide numbers aside, there are many reasons to anticipate trouble. Vietnam veterans have gone largely untreated for post-traumatic stress disorder, and many have buried those emotional wounds by drinking or overworking, said Tom Berger, executive director of the Veterans Health Council of Vietnam Veterans of America. As these veterans age into retirement, symptoms of anxiety and depression often emerge.

Troops Are Under Increasing Mental Stress

Mental stress within the military is already high. A new study by the Armed Forces Health Surveillance Center found that mental disorders are the leading cause of hospitalizations for active-duty forces. The rate at which troops are being hospitalized for mental health illness, it says, has risen 87 percent since 2000. Those who have been hospitalized have a "greatly elevated" suicide risk, the study found.

Experts such as David Litts of the National Action Alliance for Suicide Prevention believe the stress on the force will continue to rise—even with the pace of combat deployments declining. One of many reasons for this, Litts said, is that the military is shrinking because of budget reductions, cutting short anticipated careers and disrupting family plans. "A lot of people will be pushed to leave active duty who weren't planning on it," said Litts, noting that separation from friends and isolation are key risk factors for suicidal behavior.

The raw numbers of suicides are relatively small: the 350 active-duty suicides last year occurred in a total active-duty force of 1.4 million. Even the estimated 8,000 veteran suicides a year is a small percent of the 22.3 million American veterans.

But any suicide is a tragic loss, crushing to those left behind.

"You are burnt to the ground," said Kim Ruocco, whose husband, Maj. John Ruocco, a Marine Cobra gunship pilot with 75 combat missions in Iraq, died by suicide in 2005.

Combat Experience Contributes to Suicides

Recruits are screened for psychological problems and are trained to endure stress. Active-duty troops tend to be more physically fit and more purpose driven, with far lower rates than civilians of drug and alcohol abuse. They have access to virtually unlimited medical and mental health care. They are all under close supervision, hardwired into a buddy system and command structure.

For decades, these troops seemed to be sheltered from much of the stress, loneliness and emotional storms of civilian life—reflected in a lower incidence of suicide in the ranks.

But the rising military suicide rate today indicates something fundamental has changed.

Combat trauma certainly is one driving factor. For 25-year-old Andrew O'Brien, an army grunt who fought in Iraq, it was the sight of the remains of American bodies, after a convoy struck an IED [improvised explosive device], that burned into his memory and caused nightmares that eventually drove him to attempt suicide. With the help of family and a fellow veteran, he said, "I turned my life around."

A detailed study of troops' mental health in Iraq by the army surgeon general, published in 2008, found that three-quarters of young male troops, privates, specialists and sergeants saw someone seriously injured or killed; more than half were attacked or ambushed; 70 percent experienced an IED explode nearby; and 88 percent received incoming fire. One in five reported being "bothered by thoughts that you'd be better off dead" during the previous four weeks.

Some experts believe that constant exposure to weapons and carnage of war can make the idea of suicide less unthinkable. "We know what death looks like and we're comfortable with it," explained a former special forces officer who served multiple combat tours in Iraq and Afghanistan.

Noncombatants Are Also Under Stress

Even those troops who never experienced direct combat, researchers are realizing, are nonetheless experiencing the consequences of the damage war can inflict.

The study by the Armed Forces Health Surveillance Center found that for all the military personnel medically evacuated from Iraq and Afghanistan between 2001 and 2012, the most frequent diagnosis was not physical battle wounds but "adjustment reaction," a category that includes grief, anxiety, depression, post-traumatic stress and other mental disorders.

"We start off with a very healthy population," said Army Col. William Corr, a physician with the center. "Stress does cause people to become ill."

In considering the mental toll of war, "we usually think about infantrymen, guys shooting other people, but we are also seeing some problems among noncombatants," said Craig Bryan, a clinical psychiatrist and suicide expert at the University of Utah, where he is associate director of the National Center for Veterans Studies. Bryan has led numerous research projects on military suicide and has served on active duty, deploying to Iraq in 2009 to treat troops for traumatic brain injury and combat stress.

He cited the experiences of air force personnel who receive and process the war dead at Dover Air Force Base in Delaware. War trauma, he said, does affect "all those other career fields who see the consequences of war even if they are not directly involved."

"We are realizing now that a lot of service members and vets see things and experience events that are not necessarily life-threatening situations but that disrupt their sense of security, what is right and wrong—and that creates tremendous inner conflict," Bryan said.

A gradual change in the military culture has also raised stress within the ranks, experts believe. Frequent deployments have increased the isolation of those left behind. At the army's Fort Drum in New York, for instance, it was not uncommon after 9/11 [referring to the September 11, 2001, terrorist attacks on the United States] for two of the 10th Mountain Division's three infantry brigades to be gone at the same time, leaving the post a virtual ghost town.

At military posts across the country, many families have chosen to move into nearby civilian communities. More spouses find work outside the military and many send their kids to civilian schools. Under congressional mandate, underused bases have been shuttered and their military families sent elsewhere. Social media has made it easy to connect to the world beyond the military.

All of this disrupted what in the 1980s and 1990s was a comfortable, insular existence. Life in places like Camp Lejeune, the marine base in North Carolina, and the army's Fort Benning in Georgia often resembled small towns of the 1950s, with children walking to Defense Department schools, housewives gathering for coffee, families maintaining manicured lawns, and crime and drugs staying mostly outside the main gates.

"Service people used to live in their own world, and I don't mean that negatively," said Jacqueline Garrick, a retired army officer who directs the Pentagon's suicide prevention programs. "There was a protective factor to being in the military, very strong social support, a closed network."

Now, military communities are vulnerable to the same social ills that afflict civilians. The divorce rate inside the military has risen steadily—for enlisted troops, from 2.9 percent a year in 2000 to 4.1 percent in 2011. Drug and alcohol abuse rose as well through the decade; in 2011 alone, the army sent 24,000 soldiers to substance abuse programs. The number of those in the active-duty force who tested positive for heroin jumped from 45 in 2005 to 194 in 2011.

"We are not insulated from those things," Garrick said. "There is not a bubble around our military people, so that the issues of everyday life of America are the issues of everyday life in the armed forces. We are less immune than we used to be."

Whether the military's suicide rate has now passed the civilian rate is a matter of dispute among researchers. The numbers are inconclusive, said Gregory K. Brown, a clinical psychologist and suicide researcher at the University of Pennsylvania. "Let's just say it's a lot."

Early Intervention Is Important

This shift inside the military community is causing defense officials to broaden their suicide prevention campaigns to include servicemen and women who may be struggling with mental health issues, substance abuse, family dysfunction, financial problems and other issues that can be difficult to manage, but do not necessarily lead to suicide.

Many of the suicide prevention measures undertaken in the past few years, such as the highly successful national crisis line for the military and veterans, have saved lives in cases where a soldier or veteran literally has a gun to his or her head. Counselors at the crisis line are adept at talking down callers and getting them help.

Experts now acknowledge that intervention also is needed well before that point. The Pentagon's Garrick explains this using an analogy of a mountain in winter. "Life is a slippery slope, and at the top are snowflakes," she said. "Coming down the mountain are snowballs, and at the bottom is the avalanche zone where you can be buried alive. The question is,

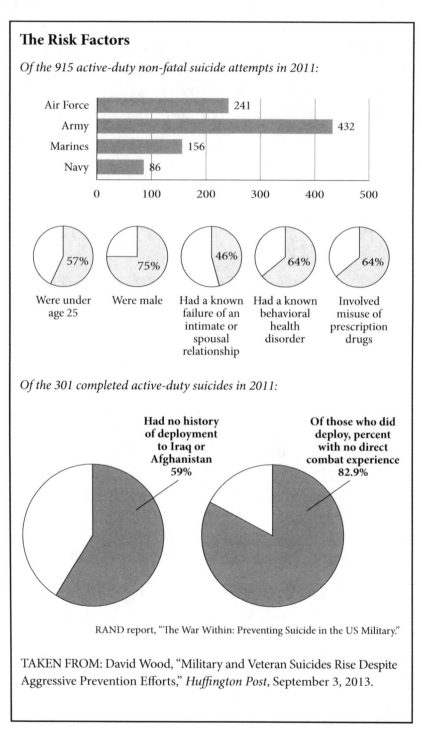

The Risk Factors

Of the 915 active-duty non-fatal suicide attempts in 2011:

Air Force 241
Army 432
Marines 156
Navy 86

0   100   200   300   400   500

57% Were under age 25

75% Were male

46% Had a known failure of an intimate or spousal relationship

64% Had a known behavioral health disorder

64% Involved misuse of prescription drugs

Of the 301 completed active-duty suicides in 2011:

Had no history of deployment to Iraq or Afghanistan 59%

Of those who did deploy, percent with no direct combat experience 82.9%

RAND report, "The War Within: Preventing Suicide in the US Military."

TAKEN FROM: David Wood, "Military and Veteran Suicides Rise Despite Aggressive Prevention Efforts," *Huffington Post*, September 3, 2013.

how do we deal with the snowflakes so they don't become snowballs and avalanches?"

Shifting suicide prevention resources to this larger at-risk group "ultimately will save many more lives," said Yeates Conwell, a psychiatry professor at the University of Rochester who has done seminal research on suicide prevention and is also codirector of the school's Center for the Study and Prevention of Suicide.

Intervening early with the at-risk population, he said, might mean early identification and treatment of mental health issues, ensuring that injured troops get the best rehabilitation so they can manage independently. The efforts can help to secure firearms at home and connect struggling soldiers and veterans with peer counselors who have had similar issues.

"What we know about suicide in older adults is that it is a complicated act" that may include many factors, but "is always associated with diagnosable psychiatric illness," Conwell said. "And by far the most common illness associated with completed suicides is clinical depression."

The problem, of course, is connecting the copious resources of the Pentagon and the VA with the troops, veterans and families who need them.

There Is a Stigma Attached to Seeking Help

For a variety of reasons—some say they just don't trust the VA—many veterans under stress don't get help. Fewer than half of all the nation's 22.3 million veterans are enrolled with the VA, officials said.

Those who do try to get help often find that the nationwide shortage of mental health care professionals translates into long lines and long waits for appointments.

"We're still having trouble getting in to the VA," said Jackie McMichael, whose husband, Mike, has struggled with traumatic brain injury and suicidal thoughts since his return from

Iraq in 2005. "Everybody has trouble getting appointments for mental health counseling." In a crisis, she takes Mike to the emergency room. But for routine counseling, "you get them for months down the road."

Even as demand is rising, there are not enough therapists trained in both military culture and suicide prevention to meet the demand, said Litts, a former air force colonel who designed the military's initial suicide prevention programs and now manages the National Action Alliance for Suicide Prevention.

"It's a safe bet that in most communities, there is a shortage of [mental health care] providers that have been trained as well as they should be to assess and manage suicide risk," he said.

The Department of Veterans Affairs recently hired 1,600 additional mental health care providers. But, Litts said, "there are only so many mental health professionals who are good and who are ready to leave their jobs and go to work for the VA. And if they pull 1,600 qualified professionals out of civilian communities, you've just taken 1,600 people who might have treated veterans in the community, where most veterans get their care. It's a zero-sum game."

As Rep. Jeff Miller (R-Fla.), House Veterans' Affairs Committee chairman, put it recently, "[L]ack of access to VA mental health care services remains a deathly serious problem for the department—one that past staffing and budget increases as well as numerous mental health summits have failed to solve."

Providing mental health care is "a huge challenge not only for the VA, but health care systems across the country—we are not always there when people need us," Jan Kemp, director of suicide prevention for the VA, said in a recent VA webinar. "Sometimes we are difficult to get to and there are long waiting lines and delays in getting services."

Once veterans do get mental health care from the VA, "we do a pretty good job," Kemp said in an interview. "What happens to people we don't provide care to, we are trying to figure it out," she said, adding that "they are at higher risk."

Within the military as well, long waits for mental health care are legendary. An army task force on suicide prevention in 2010 warned of a shortage of therapists to meet the growing demand for behavioral health care. "Although there has been some expansion in the number of behavioral health providers in all of the services, timely access to quality behavioral health care for service members continues to be a challenge," the report said.

And despite efforts to erase the stigma of seeking mental health care, many say the military culture is resistant to change. Soldiers wounded physically or psychologically tend to be cut from the herd. "If a soldier has a mental health issue and fellow soldiers learn about it, then confidence is broken and military careers unquestionably are harmed," said Dan Williams, an Iraq war veteran who said his unit ridiculed him when he sought help for what was eventually diagnosed as a traumatic brain injury from an IED blast. . . .

A Greater Effort Is Needed

Finding veterans and identifying struggling troops in time, and matching them with the right resources, is a major concern of suicide prevention officials at the Pentagon and the VA. The rising suicide numbers, they acknowledge, are evidence that a greater effort is needed.

That's why the Pentagon's office of suicide prevention is engaged in a massive effort to determine exactly what programs exist, how much is being spent on them and how they can be more efficiently coordinated. Garrick, the office director, said she has asked each of the military services this summer to report how many suicide prevention programs they have, what they do and what they cost. Answers aren't in yet, she said.

Many are convinced that the answer lies in part outside the Pentagon and VA, out in the communities where people live. Across the country, there are fledgling efforts to tackle this idea in two ways: train veteran volunteers to act as peer counselors to troops and other veterans in need, and more closely coordinate with community-based health care providers, including nonprofits. . . .

But the fact is that community programs are often fragmented, underfunded and disconnected. At the Philadelphia meeting, two officials of the city's department of behavioral health, which has an impressive array of suicide prevention programs and outreach, said they had no veteran-specific programs, did not routinely look for veterans to connect with the VA, and really had no idea where to send veterans in need.

"There are so many resources and different organizations, and one person calling one organization isn't going to get a fraction of all the help that's out there," said Valerie Glauser, a family therapist in suburban Philadelphia. "There is no community clearinghouse for all types of veteran support for those of us who work in behavioral health."

After hours of discussion, the group came up with two solid plans: spread the word about VA programs in new ways—such as posters on buses and job fairs—and train volunteer veterans for peer counseling.

With all these campaigns and programs, the most effective suicide prevention tool often seems to be an individual—a family member or a friend—who makes the effort to be available.

Army Sgt. Maj. Joseph Sanders, now 48, twice attempted suicide when depression, illness and anxiety sent him into what seemed like a bottomless pit with no other way out.

One time he put a bullet in his revolver, and when he pulled the trigger it clicked on an empty chamber—a shock that brought him to his senses. The second time he ran his car engine in a closed garage before suddenly realizing how much he had to live for.

At 1 a.m. he banged on a friend's door to ask for help.

"All it takes," he said. "You always have someone to turn to, someone that cares."

His friend took him that night to a military chaplain and then to a suicide prevention officer. "We worked up a safety plan, and they said, 'You go on home now and we'll call in the morning to make sure you're okay, and we'll call you in the evening and continue checking on you until everything is okay and you're not feeling as stressed.'"

"Well," Sgt. Maj. Sanders said. "That was quite effective."

> *"It is not the fear and the terror that service members endure in the battlefield that inflicts most psychological damage . . . but feelings of shame and guilt related to the moral injuries they suffer."*

Multiple Deployments Contribute to Suicide Among Veterans

Ed Pilkington

Ed Pilkington is the Guardian's New York correspondent. In 2012, more active-duty soldiers killed themselves than were killed in battle, reports Pilkington in the following viewpoint. He cites a study that speculates that the increase in suicides may be linked to the cumulative impact of multiple deployments. Although the US Department of Defense has launched suicide prevention programs, the suicide rate among veterans continues to grow and will likely increase as troops from Iraq and Afghanistan return to civilian life, Pilkington suggests.

As you read, consider the following questions:

1. How many active-duty service members committed suicide in 2012 compared to how many died in combat, according to Pilkington?

2. According to the viewpoint, how many veterans committed suicide in 2012?

3. What is the concept of "moral injury," and how does it relate to suicide, according to Pilkington?

Libby Busbee is pretty sure that her son William never sat through or read Shakespeare's *Macbeth*, even though he behaved as though he had. Soon after he got back from his final tour of Afghanistan, he began rubbing his hands over and over and constantly rinsing them under the tap.

"Mom, it won't wash off," he said.

"What are you talking about?" she replied.

"The blood. It won't come off."

On 20 March last year [2012], the soldier's striving for self-cleanliness came to a sudden end. That night he locked himself in his car and, with his mother and two sisters screaming just a few feet away and with SWAT officers encircling the vehicle, he shot himself in the head.

A Suicide Epidemic Among Soldiers and Veterans

At the age of 23, William Busbee had joined a gruesome statistic. In 2012, for the first time in at least a generation, the number of active-duty soldiers who killed themselves, 177, exceeded the 176 who were killed while in the war zone. To put that another way, more of America's serving soldiers died at their own hands than in pursuit of the enemy.

Across all branches of the US military and the reserves, a similar disturbing trend was recorded. In all, 349 service members took their own lives in 2012, while a lesser number, 295, died in combat.

Shocking though those figures are, they are nothing compared with the statistic to which Busbee technically belongs. He had retired himself from the army just two months before he died, and so is officially recorded at death as a veteran—one of an astonishing 6,500 former military personnel who killed themselves in 2012, roughly equivalent to one every 80 minutes.

Returning Home in Despair

Busbee's story, as told to the *Guardian* by his mother, illuminates crucial aspects of an epidemic that appears to be taking hold in the US military, spreading alarm as it grows. He personifies the despair that is being felt by increasing numbers of active and retired service members, as well as the inability of the military hierarchy to deal with their anguish.

That's not, though, how William Busbee's story began. He was in many ways the archetype of the American soldier. From the age of six he had only one ambition: to sign up for the military, which he did when he was 17.

"He wasn't the normal teenager who went out and partied," Libby Busbee said. "He wanted to be somebody. He had his mind set on what he wanted to do, and he loved the army. I couldn't be more proud of him."

Once enlisted, he was sent on three separate yearlong tours to Afghanistan. It was the fulfillment of his dreams, but it came at a high price. He came under attack several times, and in one particularly serious incident incurred a blow to the head that caused traumatic brain injury. His body was so peppered with shrapnel that whenever he walked through an airport security screen he would set off the alarm.

The mental costs were high too. Each time he came back from Afghanistan, between tours or on R&R, he struck his mother as a little more on edge, a little more withdrawn. He would rarely go out of the house and seemed ill at ease among civilians. "I reckon he felt he no longer belonged here," she said.

Once, Busbee was driving Libby in his car when a nearby train sounded its horn. He was so startled by the noise that he leapt out of the vehicle, leaving it to crash into the curb. After that, he never drove farther than a couple of blocks.

Nights were the worst. He had bad dreams and confessed to being scared of the dark, making Libby swear not to tell anybody. Then he took to sleeping in a closet, using a military sleeping bag tucked inside the tiny space to recreate the conditions of deployment. "I think it made him feel more comfortable," his mother said.

After one especially fraught night, Libby awoke to find that he had slashed his face with a knife. Occasionally, he would allude to the distressing events that led to such extreme behaviour: there was the time that another soldier, aged 18, had been killed right beside him; and the times that he himself had killed.

William told his mother: "You would hate me if you knew what I've done out there."

"I will never hate you. You are the same person you always were," she said.

"No, Mom," he countered. "The son you loved died over there."

Psychological Damage of Guilt

For William Nash, a retired navy psychiatrist who directed the Marine Corps' combat stress control programme, William Busbee's expressions of torment are all too familiar. He has worked with hundreds of service members who have been grappling with suicidal thoughts, not least when he was posted to Fallujah in Iraq during the height of the fighting in 2004.

He and colleagues in military psychiatry have developed the concept of "moral injury" to help understand the current wave of self-harm. He defines that as "damage to your deeply held beliefs about right and wrong. It might be caused by something that you do or fail to do, or by something that is done to you—but either way it breaks that sense of moral certainty."

Contrary to widely held assumptions, it is not the fear and the terror that service members endure in the battlefield that inflicts most psychological damage, Nash has concluded, but feelings of shame and guilt related to the moral injuries they suffer. Top of the list of such injuries, by a long shot, is when one of their own people is killed.

"I have heard it over and over again from marines—the most common source of anguish for them was failing to protect their 'brothers'. The significance of that is unfathomable, it's comparable to the feelings I've heard from parents who have lost a child."

Incidents of "friendly fire" when US personnel are killed by mistake by their own side is another cause of terrible hurt, as is the guilt that follows the knowledge that a military action has led to the deaths of civilians, particularly women and children. Another important factor, Nash stressed, was the impact of being discharged from the military that can also instill a devastating sense of loss in those who have led a hermetically sealed life within the armed forces and suddenly find themselves excluded from it.

That was certainly the case with William Busbee. In 2011, following his return to Fort Carson in Colorado after his third and last tour of Afghanistan, he made an unsuccessful attempt

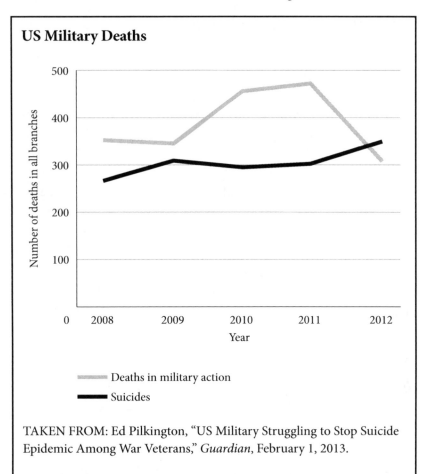

US Military Deaths

Number of deaths in all branches

Deaths in military action

Suicides

TAKEN FROM: Ed Pilkington, "US Military Struggling to Stop Suicide Epidemic Among War Veterans," *Guardian*, February 1, 2013.

to kill himself. He was taken off normal duties and prescribed large quantities of psychotropic drugs which his mother believes only made his condition worse.

Eventually he was presented with an ultimatum by the army: retire yourself out or we will discharge you on medical grounds. He felt he had no choice but to quit, as to be medically discharged would have severely dented his future job prospects.

When he came home on 18 January 2012, a civilian once again, he was inconsolable. He told his mother: "I'm nothing now. I've been thrown away by the army."

A Link Between Multiple Deployments and Suicide

The suffering William Busbee went through, both inside the military and immediately after he left it, illustrates the most alarming single factor in the current suicide crisis: the growing link between multiple deployments and self-harm. Until 2012, the majority of individuals who killed themselves had seen no deployment at all. Their problems tended to relate to marital or relationship breakdown or financial or legal worries back at base.

The most recent Department of Defense suicide report, or DoDSER, covers 2011. It shows that less than half, 47%, of all suicides involved service members who had ever been in Iraq or Afghanistan. Just one in 10 of those who died did so while posted in the war zone. Only 15% had ever experienced direct combat.

The DoDSER for 2012 has yet to be released, but when it is it is expected to record a sea change. For the first time, the majority of those who killed themselves had been deployed. That's a watershed that is causing deep concern within the services.

"We are starting to see the creeping up of suicides among those who have had multiple deployments," said Phillip Carter, a military expert at the defence think tank Center for a New American Security that in 2011 published one of the most authoritative studies into the crisis. He added that though the causes of the increase were still barely understood, one important cause might be the cumulative impact of deployments— the idea that the harmful consequences of stress might build up from one tour of Afghanistan to the next.

Over the past four years, the Pentagon and the US Department of Veterans Affairs have invested considerable resources at tackling the problem. The US Department of Defense has launched a suicide prevention programme that tries to help service members to overcome the stigma towards seeking help. It has also launched an education campaign encouraging personnel to be on the lookout for signs of distress among their peers under the rubric "never let our buddy fight alone".

Despite such efforts, there is no apparent let up in the scale of the tragedy. Though President [Barack] Obama has announced a drawdown of US troops from Afghanistan by the end of 2014, experts warn that the crisis could last for at least a decade beyond the end of war as a result of the delayed impact of psychological damage.

It's all come in any case too late for Libby Busbee. She feels that her son was let down by the army he loved so much. In her view, he was pumped full of drugs but deprived of the attention and care he needed.

William himself was so disillusioned that shortly before he died he told her that he didn't want a military funeral; he would prefer to be cremated and his ashes scattered at sea. "I don't want to be buried in my uniform—why would I want that when they threw me away when I was alive," he said.

In the end, two infantrymen did stand to attention over his coffin, the flag was folded over it, and there was a gun salute as it was lowered into the ground. William Busbee was finally at rest, though for Libby Busbee the torture goes on.

"I was there for his first breath, and his last," she said. "Now my daughters and me, we have to deal with what he was going through."

| "There's no doubt in my mind that there is a correlation between substance abuse, both alcohol and prescription drugs, and suicide."

Addressing Substance Abuse Issues Will Reduce Veteran Suicide Rates

Dave Larsen

Dave Larsen is the editor of the Fort Hood Sentinel. *In the following viewpoint, Larsen tells the story of John McCormick, a retired army officer who survived two combat tours in Vietnam, came home battling depression, and succumbed to alcohol addiction. After more than a decade, McCormick made it to a treatment facility and has been sober for more than twenty years, Larsen relates. Larsen explains that because of the direct correlation between substance abuse and suicide, it is critical that veterans be treated for alcohol and drug abuse.*

As you read, consider the following questions:

1. According to Larsen, what message does John McCormick deliver to soldiers with a substance dependency?

Dave Larsen, "Survivor: War Hero Uses Experiences to Reach Out to Soldiers," *Soldiers Magazine*, vol. 66, no. 11, November 2011, p. 13. Reproduced by permission.

2. According to the viewpoint, what made the biggest impression on McCormick at the treatment facility in Corpus Christi?

3. How does McCormick say that depression, suicide, and alcoholism can be beaten?

John McCormick is a survivor. He survived two combat tours in Vietnam and came out a hero. He survived deep depression and suicidal ideation and came out addicted to alcohol. He survived his substance abuse and came out with a message for today's troops who face the same fight: You can conquer it all, but you don't have to go it alone.

A Link Between Substance Abuse and Suicide

The 72-year-old retired army officer, a graduate of West Point's class of 1961 and Corpus Christi resident, visited Fort Hood, Texas, in March [2011], after national media outlets reported a spike in suicides among soldiers in February.

Later that month, Army Vice Chief of Staff Gen. Peter Chiarelli held a press conference at 1st Cavalry Division headquarters. With national Alcohol Awareness Month observed in April, the general discussed the correlation between substance abuse and suicide.

"There's no doubt in my mind that there is a correlation between substance abuse, both alcohol and prescription drugs, and suicide," Chiarelli, who has spearheaded the army's suicide prevention efforts, said March 28. "Suicide is a compulsive act, and when you mix alcohol or some other form of medication with individuals who may have ready access to a firearm, you have a lethal combination."

McCormick is living proof of that correlation.

"It really means a lot to me," he said, "if I can help one soldier by telling my story."

The former army officer's service record reflects uncommon heroism: a Legion of Merit, Bronze Star Medal with oak leaf cluster and "V" device for valor, Army Commendation Medal with oak leaf cluster, Air Medal (10, two for valor), Vietnam Gallantry Cross with silver star, Vietnamese Staff Services Honor Medal 1st Class, Vietnam Service Medal with silver star and bronze star, Vietnam Campaign Medal with "60" device, Ranger tab, Parachutist Badge and four overseas bars.

During his first tour in Vietnam, 1966–67, he served with the 25th Infantry Division's 3rd Squadron, 4th Cavalry Regiment, commanding Headquarters Troop. David Reed recalled McCormick's exploits—and those of his men—in his 1967 book, *Up Front in Vietnam.*

Reed discussed "McCormick's Raiders," a group of combat support soldiers—cooks and clerks, mostly—who then Capt. McCormick organized into a fighting force to ambush enemy infiltrators at his squadron's base camp in Cu Chi. He led raids several times each week over a five-month period and never lost a man.

McCormick returned in '67 a hero, and a bit of a celebrity, as McCormick's Raiders were also featured on NBC and *CBS Evening News with Walter Cronkite.*

"I use the word euphoric. I'm going home. My wife was there. My kid was there, and there were going to be demonstrators. I didn't care. They didn't spit on me or anything like that. I didn't care," McCormick recalled. "I brought a sword home from McCormick's Raiders. It's still hanging in my house."

A Different Second Tour

Promoted to major June 17, 1968, McCormick believed he was destined for great things in the army: high rank, senior command. He was what the army calls a "fast-tracker."

For the next four years, academics, in particular the French language, dominated McCormick's life: a year to study in Paris to receive three French diplomas, followed by a master's degree from Columbia University and three years teaching French at West Point.

But the war beckoned.

His second tour to Vietnam was unlike his first. McCormick served as an operations officer for a special operations unit conducting missions on the Vietnam border with Cambodia and in Cambodia itself. He flew more than 250 combat missions. Two aircraft were shot out from under him, but he survived the hard landings unscathed. Operations he planned accounted for more than 1,269 confirmed enemy killed in action.

But when it was time to return home, something was very different.

"I slept on the plane almost all the way home. I was sitting next to a colonel, and we talked about family, the war, while drinking scotch and water. We got off together in San Francisco and I went on to Corpus Christi," McCormick recalled. "I was just emotionally spent. I had no great feelings about meeting the family . . . it just wasn't there. The sense of responsibility was so intense, that when it was lifted from me, I just collapsed. I didn't want to do it anymore."

When he arrived home, that lack of emotion followed him.

"I'm sure I smiled and hugged everyone," McCormick said, "but it didn't feel the same."

After returning from that second tour, McCormick was assigned as the operations officer for a tank battalion at Fort Hood. Nightmares began to assault him. He couldn't concentrate. He couldn't function properly. He nearly lost hope.

"I sat in our home in Temple with a loaded pistol in my hand," McCormick recalled. He said he was prepared to end his own life that night in 1972. What stayed his hand was his concern that he'd somehow botch the job and leave himself a vegetable, a burden on his family.

He checked himself into Fort Hood's army hospital the next day and was sent to Brooke Army Medical Center in San Antonio.

"They didn't have all the programs they have now," McCormick said. "I didn't have much choice, I was sent. I remember walking into that ward, and it was like walking into hell. It was filled with alcoholics mostly—some old, some middle age, some younger guys. I remember they took us swimming in a pool that was ice cold. I thought, at the time, that must have been some sort of treatment. It was shocking."

Eventually, McCormick was sent back to Fort Hood and given menial supervisory tasks to perform. He avoided crowded places.

"My Legion of Merit arrived from Vietnam," he recalled. "The post commanding general gave it to me. I remember hiding behind a tree (before the ceremony) not wanting to get it."

He thought his career was in jeopardy, until orders came in 1973 sending him to the Command and General Staff College at Fort Leavenworth, Kan.

"I was euphoric again," McCormick said. "I was back on track." But four months into his studies, depression took hold once again.

"I was writing a paper about my time with special operations, and it all came back," he said.

He admitted himself to the hospital again. This time, he would bounce from Fort Leavenworth to Fitzsimons Army Medical Center in Aurora, Colo. (closed, in 1999) and, finally, out of the army, medically retired June 12, 1974.

"The next thing you know, I'm on a plane home," McCormick said. "I'm supposed to be healed, right? It didn't happen."

Through it all, the nightmares continued.

Substance Abuse Is Linked to Suicide

Research indicates that substance misuse is consistently associated with suicidal thoughts, suicide attempts, and suicide mortality. The risk of suicide is likely to be greater in persons with more severe levels of substance abuse as well as in those with depression. In addition, a propensity to engage in interpersonal violence is an important suicide-related risk factor. These findings reinforce the need for increased suicide assessment and intervention efforts to address co-occurring problems in individuals with substance use disorders and/or interpersonal violence.

Mark Ilgen,
"The Link Between Substance Abuse, Violence,
and Suicide," Psychiatric Times, January 20, 2011.

Turning to Alcohol to Forget

"They were always there. I'd just get up at night, get in the closet, close the door and pull the clothes," McCormick recalled. "The NVA (North Vietnamese Army) (is) chasing me. We've crashed and everyone else is dead. It wasn't just a nightmare, it was the same one, over and over and over."

He landed a job at an employment agency and quickly rose to office manager. But McCormick turned to alcohol, at first, just to help him sleep.

"I didn't consider myself an alcoholic," he said. "(But) it was progressive."

He lost his first civilian job. His marriage suffered.

"I'd say to myself, 'It was my disability pay. If I wanted to buy a gallon of scotch, it was my money,'" McCormick remembered. "I was destroying a marriage and didn't care. I got to sleep at night. No more closets, no more wide-eyed in bed. If you drink enough, it goes away."

"As a matter of fact," he said, "Vietnam disappeared."

Though he lost his first civilian job, McCormick headed back to the classroom and completed a second master's, this one in education. He began teaching at Moody High School in Corpus Christi. But by 1987, the booze got the best of him.

"I crashed in the classroom, shaking uncontrollably, freezing," he recalled. "I was hauled out on (a) stretcher in front of the whole student body."

Finally Getting Treatment

While in the hospital, unable to help himself any longer, McCormick said two words that would change his life forever: "treatment facility."

He was sent to a now-defunct treatment facility in Corpus Christi, manned mostly by recovering alcoholics.

"I learned humility there," McCormick said. "The biggest impression was during a group session. As we sat in a circle and they asked, 'Is there anything that happened today that would cause you to take a drug or a drink?' No."

He continues to ask himself that question every single day.

It was in the treatment facility that the nightmares finally stopped.

"I like to say that I finally made it back from Vietnam in 1987," McCormick said.

McCormick has been sober for 23 years. He's retired twice over now, once from the army and again from the teaching profession. He volunteers at the *USS Lexington* museum . . . in Corpus Christi. He remains a regular at Alcoholics Anonymous, where phrases like "Let go, let God," "One day at a time" and "Keep coming back, it works if you work it," are used liberally by its participants.

In sobriety, McCormick likes to say, "When the going gets tough, the tough get going." But, to survive, he said there's much more to it than that.

"The only problem is that when you're going through this, you don't feel tough," he said. "You've got to be able to see a future that is worth living for, be it family, job, health, anything to get out of that horrible depression."

"Depression, suicidal ideation, alcoholism—they can all be beaten, even if they happen at the same time, as long as you find something to live for," McCormick said, as his eyes misted with tears and his voice cracked with emotion. "I'm a major, retired, U.S. Army, who has been through hell, and there is light at the end of the tunnel. It can be done. It can be done."

McCormick's first marriage ended in 1990, his relationship with his ex-wife damaged irreparably. He remarried in 1995 and said he's mended his relationships with his grown children. John McCormick is a survivor. But he didn't do it alone. He had to reach out to others, and he's reaching out again.

Walking slowly to his car parked outside the III Corps headquarters following an emotional two-and-a-half-hour interview session, one question remained.

"Do you think we'll help someone?" he asked. "If we can help save just one."

"Women—particularly black women—provide each other social support and encouragement categorized by the opportunity to speak honestly with their peers."

Black Women Key to Easing Military Suicides?

Stephanie Czekalinski

Stephanie Czekalinski is a researcher at the National Journal. *In the following viewpoint, Czekalinski argues that black women have the lowest rate of suicide in the United States, while veterans of the wars in Iraq and Afghanistan are most at risk for suicide. Mental health directors speculate that the spirit of social support and encouragement that is part of the black female culture insulates black women from suicide. Suicide prevention experts at the Department of Veterans Affairs are attempting to create programs that build a sense of community and support for veterans, with the goal of reducing suicides, Czekalinski states.*

As you read, consider the following questions:

1. According to the viewpoint, what is the suicide rate for white men compared to the rate for black women?

2. How many veterans commit suicide each day, according to the author?

3. According to the viewpoint, what percentage of the veterans who committed suicide between 2003 and 2008 were white?

Black women have the lowest rates of suicide in the country, and although it's not completely understood why, Veterans Affairs officials hope to recreate elements of black female culture that may help stop military veterans from killing themselves.

Women—particularly black women—provide each other social support and encouragement categorized by the opportunity to speak honestly with their peers, said Jan Kemp, mental health director for suicide prevention at the VA. "The sense of community among themselves, and the . . . built-in support that they get from each other is something we're paying a lot of attention to, and trying to find ways to emulate," Kemp said. "I think often that veterans and men don't have that same sort of personal support, and we have to build that for them," she said. In general, white men are more likely to commit suicide than people in other groups. The suicide rate among white men was 25.96 per 100,000 from 2005 to 2009, according to the Centers for Disease Control and Prevention. By comparison, the rate for black women was less than three suicides per 100,000. Government data for suicide deaths among military personnel is not available by race. Combine that with the stress that the wars in Iraq and Afghanistan have put on troops, and the risk of suicide increases. "We're working with the highest-risk group in the nation," Kemp said. Stories abound of vets dying at their own hands after slipping through the cracks in the care network or not seeking help because of the stigma surrounding mental health issues. In April, Spc. Rico L. Rawls Jr., 22, reportedly[1] shot himself after he led Georgia state police on a high-speed car chase. At the time, Rawls was wanted in connection with the shooting death of his wife, Jessica T. Rawls, of South Bend, Ind. "My son-in-law Rico came back from Iraq a different person. We asked, pleaded, and begged for help for him, but no one listened," Rawls's mother-in-law told an Indiana TV station in a written statement. "The pre-Iraq Rico Rawls would not have done this."

In another case, Kim Ruocco's husband, John, killed himself in February of 2005 while awaiting a redeployment to Iraq, according to MSNBC[2]. "He was so ashamed of being depressed and not being able to do his job," Ruocco told MSNBC. She believes her husband was going to seek treatment, but "when he sat there and thought about what it meant to get help, how people who see you, how young Marines viewed him, how his peers viewed him . . . he thought the problem was him." Kim Ruocco, 49, is now the national director of suicide education and outreach for the Tragedy Assistance Program for Survivors, a group that provides counseling resources for suicide survivors and facilitates support groups for family members. The organization works to provide the social support similar to that prevalent among women—particularly among black women—for the loved ones of veterans and active-duty personnel who die by suicide or in combat. "We really try to provide wraparound support," said TAPS spokeswoman Ami Neiberger-Miller. Surviving family members are paired with peers who have experienced similar loss. "We give people a place where they can talk and share openly—connect with others who have experienced a similar loss," Neiberger-Miller said. The task ahead of groups like TAPS and the VA is daunting. Suicides among active-duty troops are up in the first half of this year, the Associated Press reported[3] Friday. There were 154 suicides in the first 155 days of 2012, according to AP. That was about 50 percent more than the number of U.S. forces killed in action. Last year, 130 active-duty troops killed themselves over the same period, ending June 3. Veterans are more likely than their civilian counterparts to die by suicide, according to a report published in the *American Journal of Public Health* earlier this year. About 18 veterans kill themselves every day, according to a Veterans Affairs spokesman.

Of veterans who committed suicide between 2003 and 2008, 92.3 percent were white, according to the *American Journal of Public Health*. White men made up 85 percent of the nation's veterans in 2010, according to census numbers. The VA launched its suicide prevention program in earnest in 2007, Kemp said. Since then, the crisis line has received more than 600,000 calls and 50,000 contacts via computer chat. Most contacts result in a referral for an appointment at a nearby VA facility or other services—sometimes just a ride, Kemp said. But more than 25,000 times, VA crisis line call-takers have called police because they believed a vet needed immediate intervention. Perhaps they were holding a gun, had taken pills, or told the call-taker that they could not be saved, Kemp said. Among the most important VA efforts are those that offer support between peers, she said. "People need someone to talk to—to bounce things off of, someone who perhaps has been there or knows about being there to provide that layer of hope and understanding that you can pull yourself out of this," Kemp said. "We can help you pull yourself out of this bad place no matter how you get into that bad place." Veterans in crisis and their family members can call 800-273-8255 and press 1 to talk with a VA responder. Help is also available via text at 838255 or at VeteransCrisisline.net. Families who have lost a service member to combat or suicide can also contact TAPS at 800-959-8277.

Links

1. http://www.wndu.com/hometop/headlines/Solider_kills_wife_leads_police _on_pursuit_then_commits_suicide_148006835.html

2. http://usnews.msnbc.msn.com/_news/2012/05/26/11863698-survivors-of-military -suicide-victims-come-together-to-grieve?lite

3. http://apnews.myway.com/article/20120608/D9V8R7080.html

> *"Soldiers fear that an admission of depression or trauma will make them look weak or endanger their careers."*

Big Idea: Help Stressed Vets with Sim Coaches

Adam Piore

Adam Piore is a contributing editor at Popular Science *and* Discover *magazines. Piore reports in the following viewpoint that professor of psychiatry Albert "Skip" Rizzo has effectively used video games to help soldiers returning from Iraq and Afghanistan cope with post-traumatic stress disorder. Building on this success, Rizzo has developed a video game guide designed to help soldiers dealing with depression or trauma find help, Piore states. Because many soldiers are reluctant to admit to trauma or depression, the video games are designed to provide an anonymous way for them to seek help, he suggests.*

As you read, consider the following questions:

1. What is one of the most debilitating effects of post-traumatic stress disorder, according to Piore?

2. According to the viewpoint, how many active-duty troops committed suicide in the first half of 2012?

3. What are some of the cues associated with post-traumatic stress disorder than can be picked up by Rizzo's software, according to Piore?

Grant writers and colleagues were dubious when Albert "Skip" Rizzo suggested modifying video games to help soldiers returning from Iraq and Afghanistan with post-traumatic stress disorder (PTSD). They called the idea "a harebrained treatment out of *Star Trek*" recalls Rizzo, a professor of psychiatry at the University of Southern California and associate director of its Institute for Creative Technologies. But he was convinced that the computer simulations used to train soldiers for battle could also be harnessed to help them when they returned. By immersing the soldiers in realistic recreations of combat experiences, he proposed, they could overcome one of PTSD's most debilitating effects, a paralyzing compulsion to avoid anything that might remind them of the trauma. When Rizzo finally secured a grant in 2005, his ideas were quickly validated: Three months after completing 11 virtual reality sessions, 16 of 20 test patients no longer met the criteria for PTSD.

Getting Help Anonymously

Now Rizzo is once again attempting to prove the skeptics wrong. This time he is using video game characters to overcome the reluctance of soldiers to seek mental treatment, even in desperate situations. Through the first half of 2012, at least 180 active-duty soldiers committed suicide, more than the number of U.S. troops who died in battle during the same period. According to many therapists, soldiers fear that an admission of depression or trauma will make them look weak or endanger their careers. So Rizzo and his team have created "virtual mental-health guides"—highly realistic digital mentors that deliver psychological guidance anonymously over the Internet. The guides answer questions, let soldiers self-evaluate, and encourage them to get help. "The intention here is not to replace traditional therapists," Rizzo says. "We're trying to break down barriers. Hopefully, once soldiers feel comfortable asking questions, they'll feel more comfortable accessing help."

Rizzo's characters sit across a virtual table. To begin, the words "How may I help you today?" appear in a chat box. The user may then write back, "I'm not sure if I have PTSD." The program will then inquire about symptoms and suggest places that offer treatment. The responses are tailored to what the soldier says. If the program picks up depressive answers, it might write back, "It seems like you are feeling down today. Perhaps I can recommend a website." If it senses that the symptoms are serious (for example, if someone types, "I think I'm going to end it all") the guide can refer the user to an anonymous hotline.

The first generation of the program, called SimCoach, represents a significant leap over most artificial intelligence programs currently in use, Rizzo claims. He compares his virtual mentor to Alex, a chatbot available at the top of the United Airlines website. Like SimCoach, Alex provides answers based on conversational information the user types in. But Alex cannot create answers specific to an individual. SimCoach keeps track of all the answers provided by a soldier and creates increasingly customized responses.

The SimCoach character's responses also incorporate gestures and facial expressions to convey meaning. If the guide says, "Looks like you are having a hard time," it will tilt its head to the side and perhaps hold its palms out in a welcoming gesture. "It's the only game that tracks information and builds an evolving model," Rizzo says. "The answer you get 12 steps down the line may be completely different from what someone else gets."

The Next Generation

SimCoach is being tested by several research teams at four groups of Veterans [Health] Administration hospitals and military bases. Preliminary results are positive, Rizzo says, but SimCoach is only a first step in his project. A newer version of the technology, SimSensei, should be rolled out in clinics at military bases and VA hospitals over the next year.

SimSensei can track posture, hand gestures, and vocal patterns, using those inputs to guide the computer's responses. To gain those capabilities, Rizzo added a webcam, a microphone, and Kinect, a commercial body-tracking camera used in Microsoft's Xbox 360 game console. The resulting system can recognize smiles, frowns, and affect associated with anger or depression. Rizzo's goal is to provide more realistic, targeted feedback than SimCoach can.

The newer virtual guide, while still aimed toward anonymity, will initially be contained in kiosks and rolled out for testing in crowded veteran hospitals, where soldiers and veterans now often have to wait in long lines for a counseling appointment. Eventually, soldiers will probably be able to use SimSensei at home. Already, some televisions contain motion sensors, and most webcams are capable of gathering enough information to analyze vocal patterns and posture.

Rizzo's collaborators on SimSensei include Sandy Pentland, director of the Human Dynamics Laboratory at the MIT [Massachusetts Institute of Technology] Media Lab, who has spent years studying the meanings embedded in vocal pitch and body language. To assess the reliability of reading a soldier's nonverbal cues, Rizzo asked civilians and veterans who had been diagnosed with PTSD and depression to answer questions about their symptoms, such as disturbing thoughts or nightmares.

Researchers videotaped the participants and recorded their speech patterns. Preliminary results confirm that Rizzo's software can pick up cues like gaze direction, facial expressions, posture, and fidgeting associated with PTSD.

None of this will matter if soldiers do not like working with the virtual guide. To come up with characters soldiers can relate to, Rizzo and his team showed them renderings of around 20 potential candidates before settling on the three most popular ones: Female Aviator, a young woman wearing a green aviator suit; Battle Buddy, an African-American soldier with a shaved head; and Retired Sergeant Major, a plainspoken civilian with close-cropped silver hair and a blue sweater who sits on a porch that looks out on rolling farmlands.

Rizzo believes his Sim programs are the gateway to helping more soldiers get the psychotherapy they need to overcome PTSD or depression. Hopefully, better mental health— and fewer suicides—will be the result.

Periodical and Internet Sources Bibliography

The following articles have been selected to supplement the diverse views presented in this chapter.

Jordain Carney	"How Can Government Battle a 'Suicide Epidemic' Among Veterans?," *National Journal Daily*, April 3, 2014.
Kevin Cullen	"Crisis of Veterans' Suicides Is Too Often Ignored," *Boston Globe*, May 6, 2014.
Josh Hicks	"Suicides Down for Active-Duty Troops. What About Veterans?," *Washington Post*, April 25, 2014.
Kelly Kennedy	"Voices: The Heartbreak of Veterans' Suicides," *USA Today*, July 14, 2014.
Linda Langford, David Litts, and Jane L. Pearson	"Using Science to Improve Communications About Suicide Among Military and Veteran Populations: Looking for a Few Good Messages," *American Journal of Public Health*, January 2013.
Nan Levinson	"Suicide, the VA, and Déjà Vu All Over Again," *Huffington Post*, May 19, 2014.
Leo Shane III	"Report: Suicide Rate Spikes Among Young Veterans," *Stars and Stripes*, January 9, 2014.
Travis J. Tritten	"Veteran Suicides Called 'Horrible Human Costs' of VA Dysfunction," *Stars and Stripes*, July 10, 2014.
Tim Worstall	"But There Isn't an Epidemic of Suicides in the US Military," *Forbes*, February 2, 2013.
Alan Zarembo	"A Misunderstood Statistic: 22 Military Veteran Suicides a Day," *Los Angeles Times*, December 20, 2013.

OPPOSING
VIEWPOINTS®
SERIES

CHAPTER 3

Does the Department of Veterans Affairs Effectively Help Veterans?

Chapter Preface

In April 2014, CNN released a scathing report on the Department of Veterans Affairs (VA) hospital in Phoenix, citing long wait times for appointments, the falsification of records to hide the lengthy waits, and as many as forty deaths attributable to delays in receiving care. The scandal quickly mushroomed, as it became evident that other VA hospitals were engaging in similar practices. On June 9, 2014, the VA released the results of an internal audit revealing that 63,869 veterans enrolled in the VA health care system in the past ten years had yet to be seen for an appointment. In the search for causes and solutions to the VA scandal, the concept of privatization of VA medical care—an issue that has been debated for some time—emerged as a possible solution to the problems plaguing the VA.

During their campaigns, Republican presidential candidates John McCain and Mitt Romney each put forth proposals for privatizing the VA health system. Under the McCain proposal, veterans would receive subsidies to fund private coverage for all nonmilitary medical issues. VA hospitals would continue to exist but would focus their resources on dealing with illnesses and injuries directly related to military service. As the VA scandal deepened, many Republicans advocated this approach.

The editors of the *Wall Street Journal* strongly endorse privatization of the VA. In May 2014, they wrote,

> The modern VA is a vestige of the flood of veterans coming out of World Wars I and II, but it is as unnecessary as a health-care system dedicated solely to police or firefighters. The best solution is to privatize the system. At the very least veterans ought to receive vouchers that allow them to seek subsidized care from private providers that removes the VA

as the choke point. Why are politicians punishing veterans with inferior government health care?

Supporters of the VA health system argue that the problems are caused by insufficient doctors and resources, and that once veterans are treated, they receive excellent care. Jay Bookman, columnist for the *Atlanta Journal-Constitution*, defends the VA medical system saying, "Study after study have documented the efficiency and effectiveness of the VA medical system. In almost every area, it provides equal or better care than that available in the private system, and does so more cheaply and in ways that specifically address the needs of veterans."

Other commentators argue that the problem with the VA is one of access, not quality. Garry Anderson, writing in *U.S. News & World Report*, argues that "the answer is not to create yet another health insurance reimbursement system. The answer is to adequately fund the VA health care system. VA's own internal analysis reveals that simply maintaining its hospitals, clinics and research facilities—not to mention expanding them to respond to growing needs—requires billions more than what the administration has requested and Congress has appropriated."

Charged with providing health, educational, and other benefits to approximately 21.8 million US veterans, the Department of Veterans Affairs has significant responsibilities; how well the VA fulfills those responsibilities is debated in the viewpoints in the following chapter.

> "*Most VA observers contend that the problems in the department stem from a layer of lax middle managers who are not held responsible for outcomes in facilities or groups under their supervision.*"

VA Is Broken: Death, Medical Mistreatment, Claims Backlogs and Neglect at Veterans Affairs Hospitals and Clinics

Jamie Reno

Jamie Reno is the author of the news blog The Reno Dispatch. *She was a* Newsweek *correspondent for more than twenty years. In the following viewpoint, she reports that Department of Veterans Affairs (VA) hospitals and clinics are failing to serve the millions of veterans who count on their services. Among the problems besetting the VA are medical mistakes resulting in preventable deaths, the spread of infections, and a lengthy disability claims backlog, Reno maintains. Making matters worse, execu-*

tives at VA hospitals are receiving bonuses while their facilities' performances are subpar. At the center of these problems is a culture of complacency in middle management of the VA, Reno concludes.

As you read, consider the following questions:

1. According to Reno, how many people does the VA employ, and what is its annual budget?

2. According to the VA's *Monday Morning Workload Report*, what is the backlog of new and reopened disability claims?

3. What are some of the recommendations that the author cites to fix the VA?

In May 2008, 75-year-old Jim Workman, a retired air force colonel, entered an emergency room at a Department of Veterans Affairs (VA) hospital in Biloxi, Miss., complaining of shortness of breath, coughing and fever.

A chest X-ray was ordered, and the radiologist discovered a two-centimeter mass in Workman's lung. He didn't tell Workman directly but noted the finding, and recommended an immediate follow-up in an electronically signed note sent to Workman's primary care doctor at VA.

But that doctor never bothered to look at the note, nor the X-ray. Nearly two years later, Workman was diagnosed with lung cancer. He died in January 2011.

"This should never have happened," Workman's widow, Sheila, told *International Business Times* in an exclusive interview. "Jim would have lived a lot longer if it weren't for VA. They dropped the ball. I miss my husband every day."

Sheila sued VA for failing to diagnose and treat her husband's cancer and was awarded $250,000 in March.

Frighteningly, this story is not an anomaly. It is increasingly typical of the inadequate treatment veterans receive at VA hospitals and clinics.

In 2010, Korean War veteran Gary Willingham, 80, went to the VA hospital in Dallas for what his family believed would be a short operation to remove a tumor from his neck. But the doctors accidentally clamped off his carotid artery and starved his brain of oxygen for 15 minutes. He had a massive stroke, which rendered him paralyzed and unable to eat or drink on his own. He died a year later.

Willingham's family was never informed about the ghastly mistake made by VA doctors, his daughter, Sydney Schoellman, told *IBTimes*. "I only found out after digging deep into the file," Schoellman said. "He suffered the rest of his life because we were not told the truth. We would never have approved the subsequent surgeries. They took away my father's dignity. It was horrible."

Schoellman filed a lawsuit against VA for medical malpractice and wrongful death. "They tried to shortchange us and fought us every step of the way . . . for almost a year," she said, adding that the family ultimately settled for the maximum amount, $250,000.

But Schoellman contends that it was never solely about the money.

"I wish they would push (VA Secretary Eric) Shinseki and ask him what the heck is going on at VA," she said. "No one is ever held accountable."

One presidential administration after another has vowed to fix the embattled VA, which employs more than 300,000 men and women and is the second largest department in the federal government after the Pentagon. President Obama has even increased VA's annual budget to an all-time high of $150 billion. But VA's health care system continues to worsen in more and more dangerous ways, severely underserving the nearly 7 million veterans who rely on the network for care annually.

In just the past year, we've learned about at least 21 preventable deaths of military veterans at VA facilities across the nation as well as the spread of infectious diseases at these hospitals and clinics. In addition, there is evidence of bonuses awarded to executives at troubled VA hospitals and a lengthy ongoing disability claims backlog. Meanwhile, frustrated lawmakers hold hearings on VA shortcomings, adopt new rules in hopes of turning the VA around, and even create websites highlighting VA's many problems—to no avail.

"It's become apparent to me and many others that there is a culture of complacency among the agency's middle management," Rep. Jeffrey Miller (R-Fla.), chair of the House Veterans' Affairs Committee (HVAC), told *International Business Times.* "These mid-level managers know that as federal employees there is a good chance they'll have their position longer than I will be chairman of oversight, and longer than the VA secretary will have his job. They're evidently willing to just wait out those of us who are trying to change things, and unfortunately the consequences are as serious as life and death for our veterans."

Relations between the agency and Congress have deteriorated in recent months, with many lawmakers voicing displeasure over VA's unwillingness to release reports and statistics about the agency's performance. Congress has more than 111 pending requests to VA for answers on such things as questionable spending practices, performance standards for mental health care and the breach of VA's computer network, some more than a year old, says one high-ranking congressional staffer who asked for anonymity because he works closely with VA. But these queries have been met largely with indifference and even defiance.

Preventable Deaths

Of the nearly two dozen preventable deaths at VA hospitals recently, three occurred in Memphis. One of the patients died after being given a drug despite a documented allergy to that medication. Another died from a lethal dose of a painkiller. A third died because the staff did not give the patient the proper medication.

And last week, CNN reported that at a VA medical center in Columbia, S.C., six veterans waiting months for basic gastrointestinal procedures such as a colonoscopy died because their cancers weren't caught in time. There were also five avoidable deaths in Pittsburgh and four in Atlanta.

"As we dig through the medical centers, we find that a number of deaths could have easily been prevented; it's inexcusable," Miller said.

Beyond the many deadly medical errors at VA facilities, unhealthy sanitary conditions are another scourge. For example, in St. Louis, more than 1,800 patients at the VA hospital may have been exposed to HIV and hepatitis in 2010 as a result of contaminated dental equipment, according to a posting on HVAC's accountability website. A separate report on the website claims that for nearly 18 years, unsanitary practices at the Dayton VA Medical Center potentially exposed hundreds of patients to hepatitis B and hepatitis C.

Disability Claims Debacle

VA's disability claims backlog is perhaps even more troubling because it affects hundreds of thousands of veterans. According to VA's *Monday Morning Workload Report*, the backlog of new and reopened disability claims stands at 711,775. Which is actually good news, because it is down from a peak of nearly 1 million this spring.

But what has gone unnoticed is that the number of claims that are being appealed because the veteran disagrees with VA's decision or argues that the VA gave the wrong disability rating is up: According to VA, 266,179 appealed claims are pending, compared to 182,000 in 2010. President Obama and VA secretary Eric Shinseki have promised to eliminate the disability claims gridlock by 2015.

Veterans Historically Fall Victim to Politics

Americans often glorify soldiers while battles rage and express token gratitude for their service, but quickly forget them when the guns fall silent. Since the founding of the republic, veterans have had to fight for their benefits, and their success at receiving those benefits has depended less on the country's conscience than on political circumstance and expediency. When there have been large numbers of returning soldiers, especially draftees, and they have been well organized, they have fared well. But when veterans have represented a small percentage of the population, and have been volunteers or lacked political clout, their needs have gotten short shrift.

H.W. Brands,
"What Do We Owe Our Veterans?,"
American History, June 2012.

"Veterans are waiting five years or more," for appeals claims to be heard, said Joe Moore, a partner at Bergmann & Moore, a law firm managed by former VA litigators that specializes in disability appeals. "No veteran should ever face stacks of medical bills, eviction, or other problems because VA let the veteran's disability claim appeal gather dust for five years."

Lack of Accountability

Most VA observers contend that the problems in the department stem from a layer of lax middle managers who are not held responsible for outcomes in facilities or groups under their supervision. According to a Government Accountability Office report issued in July, VA routinely rewards incompetent managers with bonuses, although they have allowed obviously poor conditions to fester and have shown little interest in fixing the problems veterans face.

"The performance pay policy gives VA's 152 medical centers and 21 networks discretion in setting the goals providers must achieve to receive this pay, but does not specify an overarching purpose the goals are to support," the GAO report noted. A May 2011 GAO review of one VA medical center found that it "did not conduct a formal evaluation of its performance award program, as required. A review of the same medical center about a year later found the identical problem."

A VA accountability website launched this summer by HVAC notes that in Washington, D.C., Diana Rubens, the VA executive in charge of the nearly 60 offices that process disability benefits compensation claims, collected almost $60,000 in bonuses while presiding over a near sevenfold increase in new backlogged claims, pending more than four months.

RimaAnn Nelson, until recently the director of the St. Louis facility where HIV and hepatitis exposure is believed to have occurred, received nearly $25,000 in bonuses since 2009.

And despite four preventable patient deaths at the Atlanta VA Medical Center, three of which VA's inspector general linked to widespread mismanagement, former director James Clark received $65,000 in bonuses over four years.

"When I see these deaths occur at VA medical centers that were preventable and people associated with that center getting a bonus, it doesn't take a rocket scientist to figure out that lower-level employees are watching all this and feel as if they don't have to be transparent either," Miller said. "It is an embedded culture."

The VA declined to comment on any of the specific allegations of mismanagement and medical mistreatment raised in this article. However, the department provided *IBTimes* with this statement:

"At VA, we are privileged to serve and care for America's veterans. We have made significant progress to transform VA to better serve veterans both now and in the future, and we know that more must be done."

The statement continued, "Since 2009, we have enrolled two million more veterans for VA health care, reduced veterans' homelessness by 24 percent, and provided educational benefits to more than one million veterans, service members and family members through the Post-9/11 GI Bill program."

What Can Be Done to Change VA?

Gene Jones, a board member at Veterans for Common Sense (VCS), a nonprofit veterans' advocacy organization, insists that VA's biggest problems won't be fixed until the agency is shaken up by layoffs and other punitive measures. "Why can't Shinseki fire more undersecretaries and other middle management types who are not doing their job?" Jones asked, while conceding that it is extremely difficult to demote or let go VA senior executives, many of whom have job protection under government employment rules.

"Maybe Shinseki needs more power, not less," Jones said.

Thomas Bandzul, a legislative attorney for the nonprofit Veterans and Military Families for Progress, is not sure that giving the secretary greater leeway in personnel decisions would help. He views VA as a rogue agency with few constraints and no one inside or outside of VA to compel the department to improve.

"If a law is passed that calls for changes, it has to be enforced, and there is no enforcement within the VA system," Bandzul said. "Necessary laws are either not implemented or ignored until the courts force the VA to comply with the law. But even the courts have extremely limited jurisdiction. Simply put, there's no policeman on the block to make VA behave."

However, HVAC chair Miller is more optimistic about his committee's ability to encourage change at VA and provide benefit improvements for veterans. He points to recent legislative successes that, for example, strengthened the GI Bill against scam artists, offered more funding for mental health care and increased coverage for burials. Miller adds that HVAC will continue to hold hearings that examine VA's lack of accountability, such as in giving out undeserved bonuses.

And Miller told *IBTimes* that he will use the committee's subpoena power if the department continues to fail to respond to requests for information.

"I'd rather not do this through the subpoena process; it puts you at odds," Miller said. "But at this point that is definitely an option. The vast majority of the 300,000 VA employees are doing a great job, but it's time we put all VA employees on notice that they are accountable. Enough is enough."

"Customer service remains the greatest strength for VA."

Veterans Are Satisfied with VA Hospitals

Robert Petzel

Robert Petzel was the undersecretary of health in the US Department of Veterans Affairs (VA). He resigned in May of 2014, one day after testifying before the Senate Committee on Veterans' Affairs about deaths at VA hospitals. In the following viewpoint, Petzel argues that the VA achieved high scores for patient satisfaction on the 2013 American Customer Satisfaction Index (ACSI). An area cited for improvement was the clarity of information supplied by health care providers, the undersecretary relates. He concludes that the VA focuses on the needs of its patients and strives to give them the best health care possible.

As you read, consider the following questions:

1. According to the viewpoint, what is the ACSI figure for inpatients recently discharged from a VA acute medical center, and how does it compare to the industry average?

Robert Petzel, "VA Rates High on Patient Satisfaction in National Survey," *VAntage Point: Dispatches from the U.S. Department of Naval Affairs*, April 16, 2014. Reproduced by permission.

2. According to Petzel, what is the ACSI number for outpatients, and how does it compare to the industry average?

3. What are the two areas of improvement needed at the VA that Petzel cites?

I'm proud to report that the Department of Veterans Affairs (VA) has once again achieved high scores when it comes to patient satisfaction, according to the independent 2013 American Customer Satisfaction Index [ACSI].

Patients Rate VA High on Customer Service

The 2013 ACSI assesses the satisfaction of veterans who have recently been patients at the VA. Since 1994, the ACSI has been a national indicator of patient evaluations of the quality of goods and services, including health care, available to U.S. residents. They review customer feedback for both the public and private sectors.

The ACSI shows how our patients evaluate us here at the VA and identifies which activities have the greatest impact on their perception of the quality of care we provide.

In addition to showing us what we're doing right, the survey also shows us where we could be making some improvements. We can use this important information to prioritize our future efforts to deliver the highest possible quality of care to our veteran patients. . . .

The 2013 ACSI index for inpatients recently discharged from a VA acute medical center holds at a strong 84 on a 0–100 scale. This is four points higher than the industry average. The VA outpatient score of 82 is within one point of the industry average.

As I mentioned earlier, customer service remains the greatest strength for VA with a score of 91. Medical providers and appointment personnel remain highly courteous with scores of 92 and 91, respectively. Medical providers are also highly professional, with a score of 90.

2013 VHA Customer Satisfaction Report on Inpatients

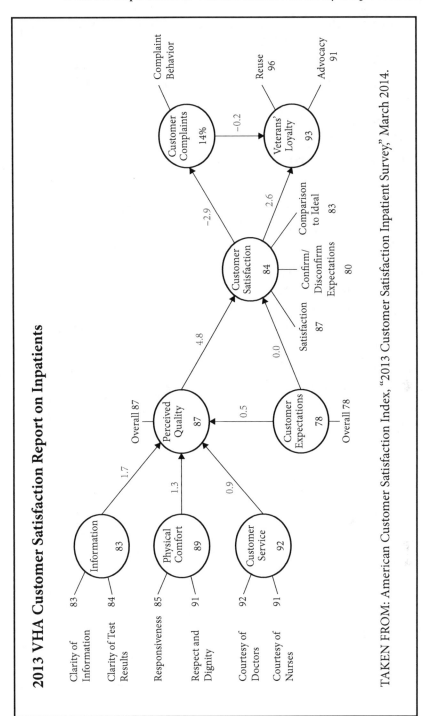

TAKEN FROM: American Customer Satisfaction Index, "2013 Customer Satisfaction Inpatient Survey," March 2014.

For the third straight year, the 2013 index of veterans' loyalty to VA-provided health care remains at 93. Respondents remain very willing to say positive things about inpatient care (91) and outpatient care (92). They are highly willing to use a VA medical center the next time they need inpatient care (96) or outpatient care (95).

Room for Improvement in Clarity of Information

The ACSI results also suggest several areas for improvement at VA. Those include the clarity of information provided by our health care providers, in particular how we explain test results to our patients; and the accessibility of VA medical centers.

We will use this invaluable feedback to guide us as we strive to make improvements in these areas.

Our work to improve and enhance the health care we provide at VA is never done. But as the 2013 ACSI survey results suggest, we are a patient-centered system dedicated to providing the best care we possibly can to veterans, and we continue to provide high-quality care. America's veterans deserve nothing less.

| *"Military veterans are dying needlessly because of long waits and delayed care."*

Hospital Delays Are Killing America's War Veterans

Scott Bronstein, Nelli Black, and Drew Griffin

Scott Bronstein is a CNN senior investigative producer; Nelli Black is a CNN producer; and Drew Griffin is a CNN special investigations unit reporter. According to a report by Bronstein, Black, and Griffin, veterans have been needlessly dying because of long waits for care at Department of Veterans Affairs (VA) hospitals. Furthermore, the investigators found, officials at the VA were aware of the problems and did nothing to effectively address them. Delays in getting care at VA hospitals have been a problem for more than a decade, they report. Additionally, there is evidence that some VA hospitals falsified documents to make the situation appear less dire.

As you read, consider the following questions:

1. How many deaths at the William Jennings Bryan Dorn VA Medical Center (Dorn) could potentially be tied to long wait times for treatment, according to the authors?

2. According to the viewpoint, what was the patient backlog at Dorn as of December 2011?

3. How much of the $1 million appropriated to solve the problem of delays at Dorn actually went to providing care for veterans on a waiting list, according to the viewpoint?

Military veterans are dying needlessly because of long waits and delayed care at U.S. veterans hospitals, a CNN investigation has found.

Delayed Care Is Responsible for Needless Deaths

What's worse, the U.S. Department of Veterans Affairs [VA] is aware of the problems and has done almost nothing to effectively prevent veterans dying from delays in care, according to documents obtained by CNN and interviews with numerous experts.

The problem has been especially dire at the William Jennings Bryan Dorn Veterans [Affairs] Medical Center in Columbia, South Carolina. There, veterans waiting months for simple gastrointestinal procedures—such as a colonoscopy or endoscopy—have been dying because their cancers aren't caught in time.

The VA has confirmed six deaths at Dorn tied to delays. But sources close to the investigation say the number of veterans dead or dying of cancer because they had to wait too long for diagnosis or treatment at this facility could be more than 20.

"It's very sad, because people died," said Dr. Stephen Lloyd, a private physician specializing in colonoscopies in Columbia.

Lloyd and other physicians across South Carolina's capital city are being affected by the delays at Dorn as veterans seek treatment or diagnoses outside the VA hospital.

Lloyd is one of the few doctors in the area willing to speak on the record about the situation at Dorn.

"(Veterans) paid the ultimate price," he said. "People that had appointments had their appointments canceled and rescheduled much later. . . . In some cases, that made an impact where they went into a later stage (of illness) and therefore lost the battle to live."

Oneal Sessions, a 63-year-old Vietnam veteran, said he was told by staff members at Dorn medical center this year [2013] that he didn't need a colonoscopy. Instead, he said, they gave him a routine test that would show whether he had polyps that are cancerous or in danger of becoming cancerous.

Sessions said the VA told him to return in several years.

But he ignored that advice and had a colonoscopy in the office of his private physician, Lloyd. In that procedure, Lloyd found and removed four polyps. Two of those polyps were precancerous, the physician said.

Had Sessions waited another few years, Lloyd said, he could have had colon cancer.

"There is a little problem that the VA had," Sessions said. "My feeling is, the VA is not doing their 'pre-stuff' that they should do to protect the veterans."

The Hospital Ignored the Problem of Delays

What happened at the Dorn hospital, however, was not just an oversight by the hospital. Government documents obtained exclusively by CNN and not made public show that the hospital knew that its growing waiting list and delays in care were having deadly consequences.

Medical investigators reviewed the cases of 280 gastrointestinal cancer patients at Dorn and found that 52 were "associated with a delay in diagnosis and treatment."

The government documents CNN obtained illustrate just how bad delays at Dorn got:

- In May 2011, a patient was brought into the emergency room needing urgent care after suffering multiple delays, and the documents state "that was the facility's first realization that patients were 'falling through the cracks.'"

- Another veteran had to wait nine months for a colonoscopy—"significant delay," according to VA records, that "would have impacted the stage at which he was diagnosed." The record indicates that by the time this veteran had surgery, his cancer was at stage 3.

- Still another patient recommended for possible disease of the esophagus had to wait four months for an appointment and 11 months for an endoscopy, at which time he learned that he had later-stage esophageal cancer. The internal VA report says that without the delay, "his cancer would have been diagnosed much earlier." And though the report doesn't say whether the veteran died, it does say that an earlier screening would have provided earlier detection "with better survival."

- In July 2011, a hospital physician sent a warning to administrators that the backlog for Dorn patients' gastrointestinal appointments had reached 2,500, and patients were waiting eight months—until February 2012—for appointments.

- By December 2011, the documents show, the backlog at Dorn had grown to 3,800 patients, according to another warning e-mail from a physician.

Little was done to effectively resolve the problems, according to expert sources and documents.

In September 2013, the VA's inspector general affirmed details of the delays at Dorn in stark language, stating that 700 of the delays for appointments or care were "critical."

Perhaps most troubling of all is that the problem at the Dorn facility had been identified, and taxpayer money was given to fix the problem in September 2011.

"We appropriated a million dollars (to Dorn) because VA asked for it," said Rep. Jeff Miller, R-Florida, chairman of the House Committee on Veterans' Affairs.

The documents obtained by CNN show that only a third of that $1 million from Congress was used for its intended purpose at Dorn: to pay for care for veterans on a waiting list.

The VA "will say, 'we redirected those dollars to go somewhere it was needed,'" Miller said. "Where would it be more needed than to prevent the deaths of veterans?"

At the same time, the documents show, the waiting list at Dorn kept growing to 3,800 patients in December 2011.

"These are real people that we're talking about, that are being harmed—either made sick, will be sick in the future or have died," Miller said.

Delays Have Been Persistent Problems

Documents and interviews show that the problem goes beyond delayed colonoscopies and other gastrointestinal procedures at Dorn.

CNN has learned from documents and interviews that other VA facilities have been under scrutiny by officials over possible delays in treatment or diagnoses.

Shortly before CNN published this report, the VA acknowledged that there have been concerns about delay of care at some of its facilities.

At the Charlie Norwood VA Medical Center in Augusta, Georgia, the VA said three veterans died as a result of delayed care. Internal documents at that facility showed a waiting list of 4,500 patients.

The VA also acknowledged that it investigated delays at facilities in Atlanta, North Texas and Jackson, Mississippi. The VA said no "adverse outcomes" because of delays were found at the VA centers in Texas and Mississippi.

CNN also has learned that, though little publicized, the problem is not new.

"Long wait times and a weak scheduling policy and process have been persistent problems for the VA, and both the GAO and the VA's (inspector general) have been reporting on these issues for more than a decade," said Debra Draper of the Government Accountability Office [GAO].

Draper's office has been reporting to Congress on the delays in care at the VA for years. It is so bad, she said, that she and her staff have found evidence that VA hospitals have tried to cover up wait times, fudge numbers and backdate delayed appointments in an effort to make things appear better than they are.

She says that just getting someone to pick up the phone to make an appointment at a VA hospital can be difficult. And getting a detailed picture of the problem is nearly impossible, she said.

"It's unclear how long it is being delayed, because no one can really give you accurate information," Draper said.

Delay Problem Remains Unsolved

Despite numerous reports and subsequent recommendations by the GAO, the problems with delays persist at VA hospitals, Draper and other experts say.

"Nothing has been implemented that we know of at this point," Draper said. "We've reported similar things, as well as the inspector general has reported similar findings . . . for over a decade."

In fact, time and time again, even at hospitals where veterans died waiting for care, administrators got bonuses, not demotions, according to congressional investigators.

The House Committee on Veterans' Affairs has created a website devoted to what investigators say shows ongoing problems at the VA, but the rewards system that Miller says is in place seems to encourage those problems.

CNN's repeated requests for interviews with the VA have been denied. Even Congress has had its requests for information ignored, Miller said.

"But unfortunately, if they treat members of Congress . . . this way, imagine how they treat the average veteran out there," said Miller. "I can imagine the grief they may be going through."

The VA said in a statement to CNN, "The Department of Veterans Affairs is committed to providing the best quality, safe and effective health care our veterans have earned and deserve. We take seriously any issue that occurs at one of the more than 1,700 health care facilities across the country. The consult delay at Dorn VAMC has been resolved."

The statement added that cases are now tracked daily and additional staff members were hired.

But sources at Dorn—both patients and medical staff—tell CNN that's just not true. The problems continue, and veterans are still facing delays that could be killing them.

> *"Do you know what happens to soldiers, marines and sailors when there is no place to turn? Check out the suicide statistics."*

Vet Determined to Share "Good News" About VA Hospital

E.J. Montini

E.J. Montini is a columnist at the Arizona Republic. *In the following viewpoint, Montini reports on a local veteran who has urged the* Arizona Republic *to soften its coverage of the controversy at a Department of Veterans Affairs (VA) medical center in Phoenix. As many as forty deaths at the hospital have been alleged to be the result of long wait times, and a secret waiting list is said to exist, according to Montini. Despite this, the local veteran says he had a good experience with the VA and that negative reports about the VA hospital will prevent veterans from getting the care they need, Montini reports.*

As you read, consider the following questions:

1. According to the viewpoint, what has been the response of Arizona representatives and senators to the problems at the VA hospital?

2. What are some of the reasons veterans fail to seek treatment at the VA, according to the viewpoint?

3. According to the viewpoint, what happens to veterans when they get no help in addressing their problems?

I got a letter this week [in April 2014] from a Vietnam veteran who has read and watched the many recent news reports alleging negligence and cover-ups at the Carl T. Hayden Veterans Affairs [VA] Medical Center in Phoenix and he is very upset about it.

But not in a way I expected.

He wants the newspaper to ease up a little on the coverage.

Really.

Negative Coverage Discourages Vets from Seeking Help

There are allegations that as many as 40 vets died awaiting medical appointments at the hospital, and that there was a secret waiting list, although the national VA says it has found no record of this.

Three Arizona congressmen have called for the resignation or firing of VA hospital director Sharon Helman and her top administrators. U.S. Sens. John McCain and Jeff Flake have asked for Senate hearings. The VA's inspector general has begun an investigation.

All of this has greatly troubled the local vet, named Terry.

Not only because it pointed to potential problems at the VA but because he believes news like this causes veterans who need help to avoid getting it.

He knows.

He was one of those veterans.

He wrote in part: "Myself, like many veterans, Vietnam, Iraq or Afghanistan did not seek treatment at the VA for a number of reasons: red tape, bureaucracy, distrust, thinking you're strong enough to overcome any problems you may be having.

"Your (newspaper's) reporting has magnified this distrust and negative feelings toward the VA.

"Do you know what happens to soldiers, marines and sailors when there is no place to turn? Check out the suicide statistics.

"Now my story: I was a serious alcohol and drug abuser for 36 years. I finally overdosed on alcohol and was hospitalized in intensive care for seven days. While I was in the hospital my younger sisters went down to the VA and got me enrolled in their 'Intensive Outpatient Co-occurring Treatment Program.' Co-occurring was my substance abuse, PTSD and depression. . . . After completing the 12-week program I continued my recovery by attending aftercare one to two times weekly for approximately a year and a half. I have been clean and sober for over eight years. I have a good job, good dog, good home and I can play golf, go fishing, camping and vacation anytime I want. That's what the VA did for me and thousands of veterans just like me."

I contacted Terry and spoke with him.

"I know that news people have a job to do but stuff like this can be terrible for some veterans," he said. "No one can predict how it is going to go for every patient who goes to the hospital, and I'm not saying some of them don't have a tough time, but the people I met at the VA were great. Really dedicated."

He worries that news articles about the VA's troubles will inhibit veterans and their families or frighten them away from seeking the help they need.

"When you're in the military you don't want to admit you need help and you'll use any excuse not to get it," Terry told me.

He had a suggestion, though. A small request.

"Try running stories like mine," he said. "I know it probably won't do much for your circulation or ratings but it might save one veteran's life."

I'd take that trade-off any day.

> *"The growing evidence suggests a VA system with overworked physicians, high turnover, and schedulers who are often hiding the extent to which patients are forced to wait for medical care."*

The VA Covered Up Long Waits for Hospital Admittance

David Zucchino, Cindy Carcamo, and Alan Zarembo

David Zucchino is a Pulitzer Prize–winning national correspondent; Cindy Carcamo is a national correspondent and Arizona bureau chief; and Alan Zarembo is a projects and investigative reporter, all with the Los Angeles Times. *In the following viewpoint, they report that there is growing evidence that Department of Veterans Affairs (VA) hospitals across the country are manipulating appointment data in an attempt to cover up long wait times for medical care. Additionally, there is a culture of reprisals within the VA that punishes employees who refuse to falsify appointment data, the reporters contend. They attribute the VA's problems to a dysfunctional bureaucracy with an insufficient number of doctors to meet the medical needs of its patients.*

As you read, consider the following questions:

1. According to the viewpoint, how many VA hospitals are there, and how many outpatient visits a year do they handle?

2. Why has the Phoenix VA hospital been at the center of the controversy, according to the authors?

3. According to the viewpoint, what do VA internal documents show about waiting times?

Three years ago [in 2011] Edward Laird, a 76-year-old navy veteran, noticed two small blemishes on his nose. His doctor at the Veterans Affairs [VA] hospital in Phoenix ordered a biopsy, but month after month, as the blemishes grew larger, Laird couldn't get an appointment.

Laird filed a formal complaint and, nearly two years after the biopsy was ordered, got to see a specialist—who determined that no biopsy was needed. Incredulous, Laird successfully appealed to the head of the VA in Phoenix. But by then, it was too late. The blemishes were cancerous. Half his nose had to be cut away.

"Now I have no nose and I have to put an ice cream stick up my nose at night . . . so I can breathe," Laird said. "I look back at how they treated me over the years, but what can I do? I'm too old to punch them in the face."

Secret Waiting Lists

The Phoenix VA Health Care System is under a federal Justice Department investigation for reports that it maintained a secret waiting list to conceal the extent of its patient delays, in part because of complaints such as Laird's. But there are now clear signs that veterans' health centers across the U.S. are juggling appointments and sometimes manipulating wait lists to disguise long delays for primary and follow-up appointments, according to federal reports, congressional investigators and interviews with VA employees and patients.

The growing evidence suggests a VA system with over-worked physicians, high turnover and schedulers who are often hiding the extent to which patients are forced to wait for medical care.

The 1,700 hospitals and clinics in the VA system—the nation's largest integrated health care network—now handle 80 million outpatient visits a year. Veterans Affairs secretary Eric K. Shinseki promised to solve growing problems with patient access when he took over in 2009, and he has been successful in some respects: Iraq and Afghanistan veterans are using VA health care at rates never seen in past generations of veterans, and a growing number of Vietnam veterans are receiving VA care as they age.

The agency reports it also made substantial progress in reducing wait periods last year, 93% of the time meeting its goal of scheduling outpatient appointments within 14 days of the "desired date."

But several VA employees have said the agency has been manipulating the data.

"The performance data the VA puts out is garbage—it's designed to make the VA look good on paper. It's their 'everything is awesome' approach," said Dr. Jose Mathews, chief of psychiatry at the VA St. Louis Health Care System. "There's a 'don't ask, don't tell' policy. Those who ask tough questions are punished, and the others know not to tell."

Mathews was put under administrative investigation in September after he alleged that long wait times led to poor patient care and what he said were two preventable deaths. He said a suicide attempt by a veteran at the facility was covered up by the hospital after a VA psychiatrist failed to provide follow-up treatment.

Several VA schedulers have told investigators that agency staffers were "gaming the system" by making it appear that appointments set for weeks or months in the future were "desired dates" requested by veterans. In fact, they said, veterans grudgingly accepted future appointments because they felt they had no other choice.

"We found people that were told to change the [appointment] dates to make it look like it was in line with VA guidelines," said Debra Draper, who was part of a team from the Government Accountability Office [GAO] that interviewed 19 appointment schedulers at four VA medical centers in 2012. The team found that more than half of them failed to correctly record the appointment date patients originally requested.

VA officials say that manipulation of wait lists has occurred only in isolated cases and that the majority of patients get timely access to quality care. VA hospitals since 2004 have consistently ranked higher in customer satisfaction surveys than their counterparts in the private sector, they note, with more than 90% of patients offering positive assessments of their care.

"As we know from the veteran community, most veterans are satisfied with the quality of their VA care, but we must do more to improve timely access to that care," Shinseki said Friday [May 16, 2014] as he announced the resignation of the VA's undersecretary for health, Dr. Robert Petzel, a departure that had been in the works before the recent revelations.

Long Waits Despite Medical Emergencies

But veterans and current and former agency employees interviewed last week described a dysfunctional bureaucracy in which turnover is high, the number of doctors is insufficient, and patients may be left dangling even when facing life-threatening health problems.

"The evidence is there. They're never going to be able to hide it," said Brian Turner, a military veteran who has worked as a scheduling clerk in VA facilities in Austin and San Antonio.

In Washington State, navy veteran Walter "Burgie" Burkhartsmeier, 73, had to wait two months to get an MRI exam at a VA facility in Seattle for shooting pains down his left arm. Eighteen months passed before someone read the MRI results—which showed bony projections on his spinal cord that put him at risk of paralysis if he were struck in the back.

In Texas, Carolyn Richardson, 70, said a VA doctor last year ordered "immediate" chemotherapy for her husband, army veteran Anson "Dale" Richardson, 66, but a two-month delay robbed him of the chance to fight the throat cancer that killed him Nov. 4.

In Phoenix, Thomas Breen, 71, a navy veteran with a history of bladder cancer, waited two months last fall for a follow-up appointment at the VA facility there after discovering blood in his urine. His family finally took him to a private hospital that diagnosed him with terminal bladder cancer. He died Nov. 30.

Six days later, a clerk from the VA in Phoenix called Breen's daughter-in-law, Sally Barnes-Breen, to schedule an appointment.

"No. You are too late, sweetheart," Barnes-Breen said she told the clerk. "He's dead."

In Nevada, Sandi Niccum, 78, a blind navy veteran, was forced to wait five hours for emergency room treatment at a VA facility in North Las Vegas last year. Niccum, who was weeping and pounding the floor with her cane because of intense pain in her abdomen, died less than a month later after a large mass was found. A VA investigation did not link the care delay to her death, but faulted the facility for the long wait and for failing to monitor Niccum.

And in Durham, N.C., two employees were put on administrative leave last week after an internal review uncovered irregularities in appointments, a local VA spokeswoman said.

Obstacle Course

© Martin Kozlowski/Cagle Cartoons.

A Culture of Reprisals

Some VA employees have said they faced reprisals after they resisted instructions to manipulate appointment books.

Lisa Lee, a medical support assistant at the VA facility in Fort Collins, Colo., said she was transferred and later put on two-week administrative leave when she objected to supervisors' instructions to manipulate appointment times. She said supervisors did not link her transfer and leave to the appointments issue; she was told instead that her performance had delayed patient care.

"They wanted me to cook the books, and I didn't do it," Lee said in a telephone interview from Hawaii, where she now serves with the U.S. Navy. "You're supposed to do your work and shut up."

After Lee was transferred, a VA supervisor in June wrote an email to the Fort Collins staff instructing them to manipulate veterans' appointment requests in order to meet the 14-day directive. In the email, provided by Lee, the official, David Newman, wrote: "Yes, it's gaming the system a bit. But you

163

have to know the rules of the game you are playing, and when we exceed the 14-day measure, the front office gets very upset, which doesn't help us."

In Phoenix, Dr. Katherine Mitchell said she could no longer keep quiet after she got a call from a fellow employee at the VA hospital there on April 27, telling her that patient appointment documents might be in danger of being destroyed that evening.

The call came in the wake of a VA inspector general investigation into the allegations.

Mitchell, who worked in the VA system for 16 years, said she went to the medical center and joined a coworker in preserving records, including paperwork that she said showed falsified wait times for medical care.

In a six-page letter, Mitchell detailed a series of attempts to voice her concerns about deficiencies at the Phoenix VA through the proper channels. Instead, she was eventually banned from submitting cases to the risk manager at the VA in Phoenix and put on administrative leave last September.

"There has been no significant change in the dysfunctional institutional culture of the Phoenix VA," Mitchell said in a statement last week. "Employees today still risk backlash for bringing up patient care issues, identifying misuse of facility resources and questioning violations of human resource policy."

Phoenix has been at the center of the controversy in the wake of reports over the last several weeks from VA employees and veterans there that as many as 40 patients had died while waiting for medical care. The VA's acting inspector general, Richard J. Griffin, told a congressional committee Thursday that a preliminary review of 17 patient deaths had not shown they were caused by treatment delays.

"It's one thing to be on a waiting list. It's another thing to conclude that as a result . . . that was the cause of death," Griffin said.

The Use of "Gaming Strategies"

Teams from the VA inspector general's office began visiting VA facilities nationwide last week to look into appointment scheduling practices and other issues. Griffin said federal prosecutors were investigating possible criminal charges at the Phoenix VA.

Officials at several VA facilities said they were committed to rooting out any improper appointment scheduling procedures and to improving patient care.

In a news conference Wednesday, Cynthia McCormack, director of the VA medical center in Cheyenne, Wyo.—which has responsibility for the nearby Fort Collins facility—said she and other managers "misunderstood" VA scheduling policies and had improperly administered them.

"We are now correcting our misunderstanding of how to schedule our veterans," McCormack said. She added that all VA employees under her supervision—as well as herself—had been "retrained on the VA scheduling directive."

Paradoxically, independent customer satisfaction surveys have consistently shown that VA patients are as satisfied with their care as patients in private hospitals.

Noble Wilcox, a Vietnam veteran from California, praised the health system for the care he had received the last two decades. He said he had no trouble seeing his primary care doctor at the VA clinic in San Luis Obispo.

"I just call and I get in in a week," Wilcox said.

Ilya Kurbanov, 28, who injured his back in a 2008 bomb blast in Iraq, said he usually has to wait six to eight weeks to see a primary care physician.

"But don't get me wrong," he said. "VA is saving my life."

The VA's internal documents show that the troubled agency has known since at least 2008 that employees manipulate the scheduling system to mask delays in care—what a 2010 memo called "gaming strategies." That memo, written by a VA deputy undersecretary, listed more than a dozen "inappropriate scheduling practices" at medical facilities dating to 2008.

Two years later, in 2012, a Government Accountability Office report concluded that the VA's reporting on its medical appointment wait times was "unreliable," outdated, easily manipulated and in need of complete overhaul.

"The bottom line," said Draper, who was part of the GAO review team, "is that no one really knows how long veterans are waiting to receive care."

"In response to allegations about scheduling and delays at the Phoenix VA Health Care System (PVAHCS), I invited an independent investigation by the VA Office of Inspector General (OIG) to conduct a comprehensive, thorough, and timely review."

The VA Is Investigating Allegations of a Cover-Up

Eric K. Shinseki

Eric K. Shinseki was the US secretary of veterans affairs (VA) from 2009 to 2014, resigning in May of 2014 in the wake of a scandal over lengthy delays to receive care at VA hospitals compounded by allegations of the falsification of records. In the following testimony before the US Senate Committee on Veterans' Affairs, Shinseki stated that VA hospitals provide excellent care, quoting a survey showing that VA hospitals score better in customer satisfaction than private sector hospitals. Despite this, the secretary said, the VA is taking very seriously allegations about scheduling and delays at a VA hospital in Phoenix and an inde-

Eric K. Shinseki, "Statement of the Honorable Eric K. Shinseki, Secretary of Veterans Affairs, Before the Senate Committee on Veterans Affairs," Government Printing Office, 2012.

pendent investigation is under way. Shinseki says that during his five years in charge of the VA, the focus has been on continuous improvement in the care provided to veterans.

As you read, consider the following questions:

1. According to Shinseki, how many people does the Veterans Health Administration employ, and how many veterans and their beneficiaries are served annually?

2. By what percentage will the number of patients within the VA's health care system increase, from 2009 to 2015?

3. According to the viewpoint, what are some of the initiatives under way to improve wait times for care?

We, at VA [Department of Veterans Affairs], are committed to consistently providing the high-quality care our veterans have earned and deserve in order to improve their health and well-being. We owe that to each and every veteran that is under our care.

Allegations Are Being Investigated

It is important to understand the size and scope of VA care—the largest integrated health care delivery system in the United States.

The Veterans Health Administration (VHA) operates over 1,700 points of care, including 150 medical centers, 820 community-based outpatient clinics, 300 Vet Centers, 135 community living centers, 104 domiciliary rehabilitation treatment programs, and 70 mobile Vet Centers. VHA conducts approximately 236,000 health care appointments—each day—and approximately 85 million appointments each year. Over 300,000 VHA leaders and health care employees strive to provide exceptional care to approximately 6.485 million veterans and other beneficiaries annually.

VA provides safe, effective health care, equal to or exceeding the industry standard in many areas. We care deeply for every veteran we have the privilege to serve. VA is committed to operating with unmatched transparency and fostering an environment that reports and evaluates errors in order to avoid repeating them in the future; one of our most important priorities is to keep our patients safe in our facilities.

That said, there are always areas that need improvement. We can, and we must, do better. VA takes any allegations about patient care or employee misconduct very seriously. I am personally angered and saddened by any adverse consequence that a veteran might experience while in, or as a result of, our care.

In response to allegations about scheduling and delays at the Phoenix VA Health Care System (PVAHCS), I invited an independent investigation by the VA Office of Inspector General (OIG) to conduct a comprehensive, thorough, and timely review. If these allegations are true, they are completely unacceptable—to veterans, to me, and to our dedicated VHA employees. If they are substantiated by OIG, responsible and timely action will be taken.

It is important to allow OIG's independent and objective review to proceed until completion, and OIG has advised VA against providing information that could potentially compromise their ongoing review. However, at the request of OIG, I have placed three PVAHCS employees on administrative leave until further notice, including two senior executives.

We will work with OIG to ensure that the need to keep the public informed is balanced with our obligation to preserve the integrity of an important OIG investigation. I have also directed VHA to complete a nationwide access review. The purpose of this review is to ensure a full understanding of VA's scheduling policy and continued integrity in managing patient access to care.

Veterans deserve to have full faith in their VA. Any adverse event for a veteran within our care is one too many. Where challenges occur, VA takes direct action to review each incident, and puts in place corrections to improve system issues and quality of care provided. We hold employees accountable for any misconduct; we incorporate lessons learned to avoid and mitigate future incidents throughout the entire health care system. VHA's first priority is to notify the veteran or their representative of the adverse event, as well as the patient's rights and recourses.

VHA is committed to a process of full and open disclosure to veterans and their families. We participate in multiple external, independent reviews every year to ensure safe and quality health care. VA will continue to develop and sustain reliable systems and train employees to prevent and detect avoidable harms before they happen. When this does not happen, we act to take necessary corrective actions in order to restore the confidence and trust in the system that serves so many.

Quality of Care

Every year, our dedicated VA employees, many of whom are veterans themselves, provide 6.3 million veterans with the excellent care they have earned and deserve. VA provides a broad range of primary care, specialty care, and related medical and social support services. We have established a record of safe, exceptional care that is consistently recognized by independent reviews, organizations, and experts on key health care quality measures. Every VA medical facility is accredited by the Joint Commission, the independent, nonprofit organization that ensures the quality of U.S. health care by its intensive evaluation of more than 20,000 health care organizations. In 2012, the Joint Commission recognized 19 VA hospitals as top performers, and that number increased to 32 in 2013.

The American Customer Satisfaction Index (ACSI) is the nation's only cross-industry measure of customer satisfaction, providing benchmarking between the public and private sectors. In their most recent, independent customer service survey, ACSI ranks VA customer satisfaction among the best in the nation—equal to or better than ratings for private sector hospitals.

Since 2004, on average, the ACSI survey has consistently shown that veterans give VA hospitals and clinics a higher customer satisfaction score than patients give private sector hospitals. Veterans strongly endorsed VA health care, with 91 percent offering positive assessments of inpatient care and 92 percent for outpatient care. Additionally, when asked if they would use a VA medical center the next time they need inpatient or outpatient care, veterans overwhelmingly indicated they would (96 and 95 percent, respectively).

Of our over 300,000 employees in the VA health care system, our medical providers and appointment scheduling personnel were considered highly courteous with scores of 92 and 91, respectively, while VA medical providers ranked high in professionalism (90 percent positive). Despite these and other favorable statistics, we know that we can always improve.

Improving and Expanding Access

The number of veterans receiving VA benefits and services has grown steadily and is projected to continue to rise as ongoing conflicts end and more service members transition to veteran status. In 2015, the number of patients treated within VA's health care system is projected to reach 6.7 million, an increase of nearly one million patients (17.4 percent) since 2009.

VA continues to improve access to VA services by opening new facilities and points of care, and improving current facilities and points of care closer to where veterans live. Since January 2009, we have added approximately 55 community-based outpatient clinics (CBOC), for a total of 820 CBOCs, and the number of mobile outpatient clinics and mobile Vet Centers, serving rural veterans, has increased by 21, to the current level of 79.

While opening new and improved facilities is essential for VA to provide world-class health care to veterans, so too is enhancing the use of groundbreaking new technologies to reach other veterans. VA continues to invest in "bringing care to the veteran"—through expanded access to tele-health, sending mobile Vet Centers to reach veterans in rural areas, and by deploying social media to share information with veterans on the VA benefits they have earned.

VA is using innovative tele-health primary care services to overcome geographic access barriers and improve the efficiency of care to rural areas. In fiscal year (FY) 2013, VHA provided more than 1.7 million episodes of care to 608,900 veterans through tele-health services linking 151 VAMCs [VA medical centers] and 650 CBOCs, as well as by connecting via tele-health with 146,804 veterans in their own homes, of which 2,284 were via video. The scope of VA's tele-mental health services includes all mental health conditions with a focus on post-traumatic stress disorder (PTSD), depression, bipolar disorder, behavioral pain, and evidence-based psychotherapy.

VHA is aggressively working to increase veterans' access to high-quality care. While we are progressing in delivering timely care to our veterans and improving the reliability of reporting wait time information, VA is committed to honoring America's veterans and there are a number of ongoing and future actions to improve wait times:

- No measure of wait times is perfect. However, with evidence from VHA's 2012 wait time study, ongoing VHA performance measures, as well as findings and recommendations from others, VHA's action plan is designed to ensure the integrity of wait time measurement data collected from our access points of care.

President Accepts VA Secretary's Resignation

President Barack Obama said [May 30, 2014] that he had reluctantly accepted the resignation of veterans affairs secretary Eric Shinseki, giving in to growing calls from lawmakers and veterans' advocates that he step down in the wake of widespread reports that VA hospitals falsified waiting lists. . . .

The president said the decorated retired army general concluded "he could not carry out the next stages of reform without being a distraction. . . . I regret that he has to resign under these circumstances."

Edward-Isaac Dovere,
"President Barack Obama Accepts Eric Shinseki's Resignation,"
Politico, *May 30, 2014.*

- VHA is constantly evaluating access and scheduling policies and technologies, and aggressively monitors reliability through oversight and audits.

- We have implemented much of this plan, and we are working to implement the remainder of the plan in the next 12 months. VHA has also instituted site visits to audit patient access to care using the electronic wait list.

Today, veterans experience primary care at VA differently than they did five years ago. VA's Patient Aligned Care Teams (PACT), the model for more personalized and team-based primary care delivery, is improving both access to health care and veteran satisfaction. Patients are assigned a PACT team that helps coordinate and personalize their care. . . .

Improving Access to Mental Health Services

After numerous military operations over almost 13 years, the state of service members' and veterans' mental health is a national priority. Meeting the individual mental health needs of veterans is more than a system of comprehensive treatments and services; it is a philosophy of ensuring that veterans receive the best mental health care possible, while focusing on the overall well-being of each veteran. VA remains committed to doing all we can to meet this challenge.

Through the strong leadership of the president and the support of Congress, veterans' access to mental health care has significantly improved. Since 2006, the number of veterans receiving specialized mental health treatment has risen from 927,000 to more than 1.3 million in 2013. Vet Centers are another avenue for mental health care access, providing services to 195,913 veterans and their families in 2013.

Since March 2012, VA has added over 2,000 mental health professionals—exceeding requirements in the president's August 31, 2012, executive order to improve access to mental health care for veterans, service members, and military families. VA has also hired 915 peer specialists, exceeding the goal of 800, to augment the work of those clinicians.

We proactively screen all veterans for PTSD, depression, traumatic brain injury, substance abuse, and military sexual trauma to identify issues early and provide treatments and intervention opportunities. We know that when we diagnose and treat people, they get better.

VA is a pioneer in mental health research and high-quality, evidence-based treatments. We strive to maintain and improve the mental health and well-being of today's veterans through excellence in health care, social services, education, and research. In the last three years, VA has devoted additional people, programs, and resources toward mental health services to serve the growing number of veterans seeking mental health care.

We are developing new measures to gauge mental health care effectiveness, including timeliness, patient satisfaction, capacity, and availability of evidence-based therapies. We are working with the National Academy of Sciences to develop and implement measures and corresponding guidelines to improve the quality of mental health care. To help VA clinicians better manage veteran patients' mental health needs, VA is developing innovative electronic tools. Clinical reminders give clinicians timely information about patient health maintenance schedules, and the High Risk Mental Health [Patient]–National Reminder and Flag system allows VA clinicians to flag patients who are at-risk for suicide. When an at-risk patient does not keep an appointment, clinical reminders prompt the clinician to follow up with the veteran.

Since its inception in 2007, the VA's Veterans' Crisis Line in Canandaigua, New York, answered nearly 1,000,000 calls and responded to more than 143,000 texts and chat sessions from veterans in need. The Veterans' Crisis Line provides 24/7 crisis intervention services and personalized contact between VA staff, peers, and at-risk veterans, which may be the difference between life and death.

In the most serious calls, approximately 35,000 men and women have been rescued from a suicide in progress because of our intervention—the rough equivalent of two army divisions. VA offers expanded access to mental health services with longer clinic hours, tele-mental health capability to deliver services, and standards that mandate rapid access to mental health services. . . .

Other Health Care Accomplishments

President Obama signed the Caregivers and Veterans Omnibus Health Services Act of 2010 into law which helps our most seriously injured post-9/11 veterans and their family caregivers with a monthly stipend, access to health insurance, mental health services and counseling, and comprehensive VA caregiver training. To date, more than 16,800 caregivers have been trained to care for our most seriously injured post-9/11 veterans. VA also has a caregiver support coordinator stationed at every VA medical center, as well as a national caregiver support line (1-800-260-3274) and website (www.caregiver.va.gov) to provide support and resources to caregivers of veterans from all eras.

VA initiated a multifaceted approach to reduce the use of opioids among America's veterans using VA health care, seeking to reduce harm from unsafe medications and/or excessive doses while adequately controlling veterans' pain. To achieve this, VHA has established nine goals for safe, evidence-based, veteran-centric pain care as part of VHA's Opioid Safety Initiative (OSI). Launched in October 2013, in Minneapolis, OSI is already successful in lowering dependency on these drugs. At eight sites of care in Minnesota, OSI practices have decreased high-dose opioid use by more than 50 percent.

OSI places an emphasis on patient education, close patient monitoring with frequent feedback, and complementary and alternative medicine practices like acupuncture. These . . . pain management guidelines encourage the use of other medications and therapies in lieu of habit-forming opiates. OSI is an example of VHA's personalized, proactive and patient-centered approach to health care through an innovative and comprehensive plan that monitors dispensing practices system wide, includes patient and provider education, testing and tapering programs, and alternative therapies like behavior therapy.

Focus on Continuous Improvement

These accomplishments are the results of VA's focus over the past five years—during which time we have worked to increase veterans' access to high-quality health care, education and training, and employment opportunities in both the public and private sectors. There is always more work to do, and VA is focused on continuous improvement to the care we provide to our nation's veterans.

I appreciate the hard work and dedication of VA employees, our partners from veterans' service organizations—important advocates for veterans and their families—our community stakeholders, and our dedicated VA volunteers. I also respect the important role Congress and the dedicated members of this committee [Senate Committee on Veterans' Affairs] play in serving our veterans, and I look forward to continuing our work with Congress to better serve them all. Again, thank you for the opportunity to appear before you today and for your unwavering support of those who have served this great nation in uniform.

Periodical and Internet Sources Bibliography

The following articles have been selected to supplement the diverse views presented in this chapter.

H.W. Brands	"What Do We Owe Our Veterans?," *American History*, June 2012.
Jordain Carney	"The VA Scandal Just Keeps Spreading," *National Journal*, July 14, 2014.
Bob Confer	"VA Hospitals: Everything That's Wrong with Government Healthcare," *New American*, January 14, 2013.
James Dao	"Veterans Wait for Benefits as Claims Pile Up," *New York Times*, September 27, 2012.
Amy Davidson	"A Tough Report on the V.A. Waiting-List Scandal," *New Yorker*, May 28, 2014.
Josh Hicks	"VA Hospitals on Par with Private Sector for Patient Satisfaction," *Washington Post*, April 17, 2014.
Anna Mulrine	"Veterans' Benefit? VA, Buried Under Claims, Says It's Finally Digging Out," *Christian Science Monitor*, July 4, 2013.
Richard A. Oppel Jr.	"American Legion, Citing Problems, Calls for Veterans Secretary to Resign," *New York Times*, May 7, 2014.
Elaine Quijano	"Officials at Troubled VA Hospitals Received Big Bonuses," CBS News, August 27, 2013.
Sally Satel and Michael H. McLendon	"Hospitals Aren't the VA's Only Scandal," *Boston Globe*, June 15, 2014.
Katie Zezima	"Everything You Need to Know About the VA—and the Scandals Engulfing It," *Washington Post*, May 30, 2014.

CHAPTER 4

How Effective Are the Government's Education Programs for Veterans?

Chapter Preface

In 1932, World War I veterans marched on Washington in the Bonus March, demanding compensation that had been promised them. With this memory fresh in mind as World War II was winding down, politicians and advocates for veterans were determined that this war's veterans would receive better treatment than the veterans of the previous war.

Concerned that when the more than fifteen million men and women serving in the armed forces returned home widespread unemployment would result, in 1943 the National Resources Planning Board recommended the creation of educational and training programs for veterans. Although six hundred separate bills came before Congress, legislators failed to pass any of them. It wasn't until the American Legion got involved that the GI Bill, or the Servicemen's Readjustment Act, became reality. Composed primarily of World War I veterans, the American Legion was appalled by the shabby treatment given to the veterans of the First World War. Harry W. Colmery, an attorney and former commander of the American Legion, crafted what would become the GI Bill, and the American Legion mounted an aggressive campaign to ensure its passage.

The GI Bill, signed into law by President Franklin D. Roosevelt on June 22, 1944, provided up to four years of college or training; a monthly allowance while attending college; federally guaranteed home, farm, and small business loans; and unemployment benefits for up to one year to veterans of World War II. The bill played a key role in building what President Barack Obama called in 2014 "the greatest middle class the world has known."

In the first seven years of the GI Bill, 7.8 million veterans received educational benefits—2.3 million attended college, the remainder received vocational or on-the-job training. The number of college degrees awarded more than doubled from 1940 to 1950, and in 1947, 49 percent of those enrolled in colleges were veterans. When the educational component of the original GI Bill expired in 1956, approximately $14.5 billion had been paid out in educational benefits. However, the Department of Veterans Affairs estimates that that amount was more than covered by the income taxes paid by a better educated workforce. The GI Bill has been extended several times—in 1952, to cover approximately 2.3 million Korean War veterans, and in 1966 and 1972 to cover approximately 8 million Vietnam veterans. The most recent GI Bill, the Post-9/11 Veterans Educational Assistance Act, more commonly known as the Post-9/11 GI Bill, was signed into law on June 30, 2008. It is more generous than its predecessors, providing enhanced educational benefits, living allowances, funds for books and materials, and the ability to transfer benefits to a spouse or child.

Although the concept of providing educational benefits for veterans has historically been popular, many veterans' groups argue that the execution of the program through the Department of Veterans Affairs is lacking. In the following chapter, commentators debate the effectiveness of government-sponsored programs for veterans' education.

> *"After the Post-9/11 GI Bill extended benefits to hundreds of thousands more veterans, benefit use skyrocketed in many places."*

More Veterans Taking Advantage of Post-9/11 GI Bill

Lauren Kirkwood

Lauren Kirkwood is a Washington, DC, reporting intern for McClatchy newspapers. In the following viewpoint, Kirkwood reports that the enactment of the Post-9/11 GI Bill, which provides up to thirty-six months of education benefits to veterans, is responsible for a 67 percent increase in veterans attending college. Several outreach centers have been set up at colleges, including ones at Clemson University and the University of Georgia, and are designed to provide veterans with information about the resources available to them as well as to create a social support network among veterans, the author explains.

As you read, consider the following questions:

1. According to the viewpoint, how many veterans were attending college in 2012 compared to 2009?

2. What are some of the tools that the VA has designed to make it easier for veterans to use their education benefits, according to Kirkwood?

3. What was the growth percentage of education beneficiaries in Virginia from 2009 to 2012, according to the viewpoint?

In the year since Clemson University launched its Student Veterans Success Center, its volunteer staff has worked to transform the small alcove in the School of Computing into a place where those transitioning from military to civilian life can connect with their peers.

Post-9/11 GI Bill Is Responsible for Enrollment Increases

"It's not just a physical space for vets, it's a place they can come and relax, they can meet other vets, they can create that social support network," said Benjamin Curtis, president of the Clemson Student Veterans Association in Clemson, S.C. "Coming back from a social network that's so strong with the military, you kind of lose all that."

The need for such support centers has jumped in recent years as every U.S. state has seen a rise in the number of veterans using education benefits from the Department of Veterans Affairs [VA].

Since the Post-9/11 GI Bill [Post-9/11 Veterans Educational Assistance Act] was fully enacted in 2009, South Carolina, for example, saw the number of such students increase 89 percent, according to an analysis of VA data.

Nationwide, the increase from fiscal 2009 to fiscal 2012—the last year data was available—was 67 percent, from 564,487 students to 945,052.

Nearby states also saw increases: North Carolina, 71 percent; Florida, 73 percent; and Georgia, 76 percent.

The Post-9/11 GI Bill was originally passed in 2008. It extended education benefits to service members who have been on active duty 90 or more days since Sept. 10, 2001, or who were discharged with a service-related disability after 30 days. It provides up to 36 months of education benefits, generally payable for 15 years following release from active duty.

A provision of the Post-9/11 GI Bill also allows veterans and service members to transfer unused benefits to their children or spouses, but about 79 percent are benefits used by veterans or service members themselves, according to VA data.

Curtis Coy, VA's deputy undersecretary for economic opportunity, called the Post-9/11 GI Bill the most generous veterans benefit program since the original 1944 GI Bill, which provided benefits for returning World War II veterans. He said the program's generosity is likely fueling the big increases.

VA Makes It Easier for Veterans to Understand Benefits

The VA has recently created several tools designed to make it easier for veterans to pursue higher education.

A new online complaint system, launched in January, allows student veterans to detail problems they've experienced trying to access benefits at certain universities; some schools have been accused of using deceptive tactics to boost veteran enrollment.

An online "GI Bill Comparison Tool," meanwhile, allows veterans to easily compare how they can use their benefits at different universities.

On the state level, many colleges and universities have worked to improve student veterans' access to crucial resources. Those schools play an important role in ensuring veterans get what they're due, and they should maintain their efforts to assist veterans as more come back from overseas, said Paul Rieckhoff, founder and CEO [chief executive officer] of the advocacy group Iraq and Afghanistan Veterans of America.

"As we approach the 11th anniversary of the war in Iraq and as the war in Afghanistan winds down, our outreach efforts should intensify, not abate," Rieckhoff said. "Colleges and universities need to better understand the different facets of GI Bill benefits and help raise awareness about veterans' education benefits."

In Virginia, where the number of education beneficiaries rose 144 percent from 2009 to 2012, George Mason University's Office of Military Services holds sessions during freshman and transfer-student orientations to help veterans understand their GI Bill benefits. It also produces a monthly newsletter for student veterans at the campus in Fairfax, in suburban Washington, said Walter Sweeney, assistant transition coordinator at the office. The office also doubles as a student lounge where vets can do homework, eat lunch or relax between classes, he said.

Similarly, at the University of Georgia in Athens, a Student Veterans Resource Center provides assistance with VA benefits certification, health care, counseling, disability services, tutoring and advising. It also serves as a place for student veterans to connect with one another, said Charles T. Barco, who directs the center.

Before 2010, the number of veterans using education benefits rose modestly each year in most states. In South Carolina, the number of beneficiaries hit 7,000 in 2001, rising slowly to 7,872 by 2009.

But after the Post-9/11 GI Bill extended benefits to hundreds of thousands more veterans, benefit use skyrocketed in many places. By 2010, the number of beneficiaries in South Carolina was 13,056, according to VA records.

A Support Network Creates a Sense of Community

Members of Clemson's Student Veterans Association have worked to increase outreach to veterans at the university by

Education Is More Important than Ever

The GI Bill [referring to the Servicemen's Readjustment Act] was approved just weeks after D-Day, and carried with it a simple promise to all who had served: You pick the school, we'll help pick up the bill. And what followed was not simply an opportunity for our veterans—it was a transformation for our country. By 1947, half of all Americans enrolled in college were veterans. . . .

We owe the same obligations to this generation of servicemen and women, as was afforded that previous generation. That is the promise of the Post-9/11 GI Bill. It's driven by the same simple logic that drove the first GI Bill—you pick the school, we'll help pick up the bill. . . .

And this is even more important than it was in 1944. The first GI Bill helped build a post-war economy that has been transformed by revolutions in communications and technology. And that's why the Post-9/11 GI Bill must give today's veterans the skills and training they need to fill the jobs of tomorrow. Education is the currency that can purchase success in the 21st century, and this is the opportunity that our troops have earned.

Barack Obama, "Remarks by the President on the Post-9/11 GI Bill," August 3, 2009.

volunteering to staff the veterans' support center a few hours a week. They do so between classes and other responsibilities, said Curtis, who served in the Marine Corps for nine years.

"The idea is to create a focal point where any student veteran can come and get information about everything ranging from financial aid to dealing with the VA and support services," he said.

At its peak, Curtis said, about 20 to 30 student veterans were volunteering an hour or two a week to keep the center open. That number has dwindled, as many veterans are juggling schoolwork, jobs and families, he said.

The Student Veterans Association hopes to secure a larger space for the center soon, and it wants to establish a relationship with a faculty member who could serve as a voice for student veterans to the administration. Small policy changes—such as automatic excused absences from class when a student has a VA appointment—are also on the association's agenda, Curtis said.

Because Clemson does not track students' veteran status, the Student Veterans Association has no way of knowing exactly how many veterans are attending the university or of easily contacting all of them, Curtis said.

According to the VA's comparison tool, which shows how many students receive VA benefits at universities across the country, 498 Clemson students are using GI Bill benefits.

Members of the Student Veterans Association are working with Clemson officials to make it possible for students to identify themselves as veterans on their student records, Curtis said; that would make it much easier to let student vets know about resources on the campus.

Those resources include help with filling out GI Bill paperwork, a process with which student veterans are often unfamiliar, Curtis said. Centers like his also create a sense of community among a student population whose members often live off campus and may not be as involved with other campus organizations, he said.

"It makes life so much easier to have a place and somebody who can guide you through it," he said.

"There were thousands more [veterans] just like me all over the country who were losing houses, cars, and much more."

Poor Administration of the Post-9/11 GI Bill Leaves Veterans Strapped for Cash

Tyler Bradley

A veteran of the US Army, Tyler Bradley is a student at Linn-Benton Community College. In the following viewpoint, taken from the college's student-run newspaper, the Commuter, *Bradley relates his experience with the Post-9/11 GI Bill. Although he was delighted with the generosity of the bill, he was discouraged by the execution of the program through the Department of Veterans Affairs (VA). Bradley reports that the VA claimed that a higher enrollment than anticipated was responsible for the delay in benefits and that thousands of veterans around the country suffered as a result.*

As you read, consider the following questions:

1. What benefits was the author to receive under the Post-9/11 GI Bill?

2. What complaints does the author have about the way that the VA handled the situation of late payments?

3. How does the author know that other veterans didn't fare as well as he did?

With an optimistic smile on my face and a belly full of confidence I was departing the main gate of Fort Lewis, Washington, for the last time. I was headed down the Yellow Brick Road—15 South out of Tacoma—and on to the land of milk and honey—LBCC [Linn-Benton Community College]— where I would cash in on my hard-earned benefit of free schooling that I had been fantasizing about for years. Through the Post-9/11 GI Bill [Post-9/11 Veterans Educational Assistance Act] and the [Department of] Veterans Affairs [VA] I would get free tuition for 36 months of college on top of a juicy $1500 a month housing allowance[; this] was something that seemed too good to be true. Not since my early days of puberty had I spent so many hours lusting over my own thoughts. Brimming with joyful academic piss and vinegar, I moved my girlfriend and myself into a de-lux apartment in South Salem and ventured boldly into the wondrous world of winter semester at LBCC.

Promised Funds Were Delayed

Jul. 17, 2012: Broke, bitter, and in imminent danger of eviction, the young, exuberant, hopeful college student I used to be had transformed into a brittle shell of the man I once was. I had fallen from veteran patriot to subversive protester. I was going to storm the halls of Congress, American flag in hand, and engage in a brisk bout of fisticuffs with the man or woman responsible for my digression. Well maybe not, but I was not very happy. Here it was, weeks after the rent was due on the first of the month and I was left sitting with no housing allowance in sight, and the only thing that I had to present to the landlord was a pile of excuses from the VA. For those of

Post-9/11 GI Bill Is Not Working

[The Post-9/11 GI Bill] has failed to deliver on its promise for tens of thousands of young veterans, according to interviews with students and administrators. Student veterans from across the country report that the Department of Veterans Affairs simply hasn't paid their tuition yet this semester, or that it just arrived, months late. Promised housing stipends, too, remain unpaid.

Rosie Gray, "For Thousands of Veterans,
the New G.I. Bill Isn't Working,"
BuzzFeed, March 8, 2012.

you who have not yet paid rent on your own, know that landlords do not accept excuses for payment. The lady that I talked to from the VA seemed to think they might, but I tried. They didn't. It must be a West Coast thing?

With no rent payment in sight and all of my bills mounting, I did what every young boy dreams of doing when he grows up to be a strong, independent, young man: Beg for money from nonprofits. I had gone from the badass Rambo, double-fisting M60s, crashing through jungles, blowing people's faces off left and right to the crying, cold, slobbering, vagrant Rambo in the sad parts of *First Blood*—the one that the cops call a hippie and spray down with the hose. I was scared of cops for a bit.

The worst part about all of this was that I was not the only one in this predicament. There were thousands more just like me all over the country who were losing houses, cars, and much more. Men and women who had given much more than me, and deserved much more than an eviction notice from a landlord and a bucket full of excuses from the VA. I was lucky, however, because my only worry was to pay the rent and other bills. I did not have a family to support from the money that we all rely on through the Veterans Affairs and the Post-9/11 GI Bill.

Increased Enrollment Blamed for Late Payments

The VA had released a few official statements that pinned the blame on the late payments due to an increase in student enrollment and the start of a new program, but these explanations came weeks after many vets had been without their housing allowances, and the VA still had no form of assistance to veterans who were left in a hard spot because of the backup.

I finally ended up receiving my housing allowance the day before my eviction hearing, so I escaped this situation relatively unscathed. Other veterans have not fared so well. The Post-9/11 GI Bill's Facebook page is crawling with veterans who are responding with some pretty harsh words to the VA's postings about the lateness of payments. Major news networks have also covered the lapse in payments, and Congress has recently become aware of the issues with the Post-9/11 GI Bill's recent bouts of infidelity.

I am extremely grateful for the benefits that I am entitled to and the treatment that I receive as a veteran in this country, and I realize people should have a sizeable financial buffer to carry them through issues such as this. However, I also realize that this has been a continuing problem for the many great men and women who gave a tremendous portion of their lives to their country when so much of America was not willing or able to. Excuses and reasons aside, this issue must be addressed and fixed permanently to serve those who have already.

"Proponents of the [Post-9/11 GI Bill] overlooked one crucial issue: Who determines in-state residency?"

Residency Requirements Leave Veterans in Some States with High Tuition Bills

Peter Galuszka

Peter Galuszka is a journalist and author who is the principal of Galuszka Associates. In the following viewpoint, Galuszka argues that although the Post-9/11 GI Bill provides more generous educational benefits than its predecessor did, the bill failed to specify consistent residency requirements among states. As a result, residency requirements are interpreted inconsistently from state to state, and some veterans are compelled to pay more if they don't qualify for in-state tuition, he explains. A bill requiring states to charge veterans in-state tuition regardless of whether or not they meet residency requirements was passed by the US House of Representatives in February of 2014 and was referred to the US Senate Committee on Veterans' Affairs.

Peter Galuszka, "Caught in the Gap," *Diverse: Issues in Higher Education*, February 27, 2014, pp. 42–44. www.diverseeducation.com. Copyright © 2014 by Diverse: Issues in Higher Education. All rights reserved. Reproduced by permission.

As you read, consider the following questions:

1. According to the viewpoint, what are the benefits under the Post-9/11 GI Bill?

2. According to the author, how many veterans will muster out of the service each year from 2014 to 2019?

3. How many states readily grant in-state status easily, according to Galuszka?

In 2008, Hayleigh Perez, an Iowa native and Iraq War veteran, decided to lay down roots in North Carolina. Stationed at Fort Bragg, the army radiological technician had just married another soldier, Jose Perez-Rodriquez. They bought a house in Raeford not far from the base but were soon moving again.

Inconsistent Rules

Perez's husband was transferred to a recruitment post in Waco, Texas. She had orders to follow him to Fort Hood nearby. While living in Texas, they kept up their property taxes and drivers' licenses in North Carolina, where they intended to settle permanently.

Perez left military service in 2009 and returned to North Carolina in 2012 in advance of her husband's upcoming transfer back to Fort Bragg. After her military discharge, Perez had studied in Texas and wanted to finish some course work in North Carolina so she could pursue a career as a physician's assistant. To her amazement, the University of North Carolina [UNC] at Pembroke denied her in-state residency status.

"It was the beginning of a nightmare," said Perez.

Fayetteville State University granted her residency, but she preferred courses at UNC Pembroke. That meant paying more than $4,300 out of her pocket. She stayed at the university for a semester but was so frustrated with the school that she launched her own campaign for veterans' rights, collecting more than 145,000 signatures on a protest petition to the North Carolina legislature and board of governors of the University of North Carolina system and filing a lawsuit that was later dismissed on jurisdictional grounds.

Her problem resulted from a catch in the so-called Post-9/11 GI Bill [Post-9/11 Veterans Educational Assistance Act] that was passed in 2008 to replace the less generous Montgomery bill of 1982, which provided $1,648 a month for 36 academic months and possibly more.

"The 9/11 bill was an improvement because it expanded benefits," said Chris Cate, vice president for research at the Student Veterans of America.

Who's a Resident?

The post-9/11 bill covers all tuitions and fees up to the full cost of in-state tuition. It is also more flexible, and benefits can be transferred to children of active-duty personnel, others note. Proponents of the post-9/11 bill overlooked one crucial issue: Who determines in-state residency? It turned out that the states would do so but would act without any specific standards.

Angry veterans found they could owe $10,000 or more a year to make up the difference between in-state and out-of-state fees. The issue takes on added significance because some 250,000 veterans will muster out of service each year for the next five years as military activity in Iraq and Afghanistan winds down.

As the veterans' outcry has grown louder, some states are becoming more lenient albeit on a piecemeal basis. At first, only about six states granted in-state status easily. Now about 20, including Arizona, Colorado, Virginia and Ohio, do so. Two bills are pending before Congress that would either mandate in-state status to veterans automatically or require states to grant residency if a veteran can show a driver's license or other relevant identification.

In some states, veterans have had few snags with the residency issue. Sgt. Hiram Pritchard, a helicopter crew chief with the Virginia National Guard who had served in Iraq with the regular army, said he had no problems with veterans' benefits as he takes courses at a local community college in the Richmond area to prepare for a degree in civil engineering.

Pritchard talked as he set up an exhibition of military uniforms and equipment at Byrd Park in Richmond where 59 vendors were readying booths to provide local veterans with information last Veterans Day [of 2013]. He got most of his benefits under the earlier Montgomery bill, but said that the post-9/11 bill "is a great bill" and that Virginia is fairly lenient about allowing in-state tuition.

However, not all states have been so accommodating after their tax revenue streams have run dry during the most recent recession. The post-9/11 bill was passed before the unexpected recession that made it harder for states to bear the cost of allowing veterans to pay tuition as in-state residents. Some states became less lenient with granting in-state status or applied rules inconsistently.

The conundrum is especially acute in North Carolina, where Tar Heel intransigence has spawned the creation of special veterans' groups to fight for education rights and has even prompted one veteran, Jason Thigpen of Holly Ridge, to run for Congress as a Democrat in North Carolina's 3rd District. Thigpen, a graduate of UNC Wilmington, founded the Student Veterans Advocacy Group to lobby for veterans' benefits.

Thigpen, who was wounded in an explosion in Iraq, said the post-9/11 bill has some good features, such as allowing active-duty personnel to use benefits for their children. He wonders "why weren't the colleges and community colleges talking to the vets about major changes in residencies" before the bill was passed.

He said he's especially surprised that North Carolina would be so chintzy about determining in-state residency. Ironically, the state has more than 400,000 jobs dependent upon the military, six major installations and about 150,000 active-duty personnel.

"The state of North Carolina has mandated itself as being the most military-friendly state, and you got to see just how friendly they really were," he noted. So far, the Student Veterans Advocacy Group in which Thigpen and Perez are involved has represented 40 veterans in disputed residency cases.

Paying the Tab

Cost to the state is a big issue, Thigpen said. If North Carolina were more lenient, it might have to pick up from $50 million to $150 million a year to help pay for all the veterans who want to stay in North Carolina, he said.

Passing along costs to the states is precisely the problem, said Barmak Nassirian, director of federal relations and policy analysis at the American Association of State Colleges and Universities in Washington, D.C.

"Of course, this is of enormous interest and a moral obligation for our veterans," said Nassirian, but the problem, he added, is more complex.

One reason why some states have made in-state tuition available, making up the difference in VA benefits for education, is based on a legacy idea that the veterans' families may have been in the state for decades helping to pick up the tab by paying taxes. If there's a federal mandate to force in-state tuition for all veterans, "Congress is essentially legislating a financial free lunch," he said. "It's a problem of arithmetic. It doesn't pay the bills."

One bill, the [GI Bill] Tuition Fairness Act of 2013, introduced by U.S. Rep. Jeff Miller, R-Fla., chairman of the House Committee on Veterans' Affairs, would require states to charge in-state tuition for veterans with no compensation from the federal government to make up the difference.

Another bill introduced by U.S. Rep. G.K. Butterfield, D-N.C., would increase federal spending to help students by allowing out-of-state veterans attending public institutions to receive up to $18,000 in education benefits, Nassirian said. It would cost from $1.1 billion to $1.5 billion over 10 years, according to the Congressional Budget Office. It could be of immediate help to up to 20,000 veterans, said Kezmiche Atterbury, communications director for Butterfield.

The Miller bill has moved out of committee as a compromise is hammered out about federal monetary support and applying some time limits on eligibility, a staff member on the Veterans' Affairs Committee who spoke on background said. [Editor's note: The Miller bill passed in the House of Representatives on February 4, 2014, and was sent to the Senate.]

Relief will come too late for many veterans like Perez. She said her treatment by UNC Pembroke was "hateful and humiliating." She appealed to the UNC system board of governors and paid the tuition difference. At one point, Perez said she was told that she was not a state resident because her husband hadn't arrived back in North Carolina although he had army orders to return to Fort Bragg.

Eventually, she went on to the state capital in Raleigh to the board of the UNC school system but faced a "hostile environment" and was hamstrung by what she said were petty ploys by UNC Pembroke such as sending information packets for her appeals that did not include some of her residency documents.

Sandy Briscar, spokeswoman for UNC Pembroke, said that the UNC system board determined that the school "handled the residency issue the right way." She declined to speak in detail about the Perez case unless Perez gave written permission, which Perez declined to do.

Perez, meanwhile, completed college online, earning degrees from Thomas Edison State College in New Jersey and Liberty University in Virginia. She received her master's in public policy from Liberty. She has given up on becoming a physician's assistant and plans to work on public policy issues.

States like North Carolina only hurt themselves when "they drive veterans away," said Perez, who will be leaving the Tar Heel State with her husband, who is being transferred to Fort Wainwright, Alaska.

"We are going to cut ties because of this education business," she said.

> *"For-profit and community colleges continue to dominate the list of the top institutions where veterans use their education benefits."*

Many Veterans Prefer to Attend For-Profit and Community Colleges

Michael Sewall

Michael Sewall is a custom content director at Patch.com and was an editorial intern at the Chronicle of Higher Education. *In the following viewpoint, Sewall argues that for-profit and community colleges were the most popular choices of veterans using benefits from the Post-9/11 GI Bill in academic 2009–2010, the first year the benefits were available. Of the fifteen institutions that enrolled more than one thousand students under this program, twelve were for-profit or community colleges, he states. The factors influencing college of choice are cost, convenience, geography, and support systems, according to the officials and veterans Sewall cites.*

As you read, consider the following questions:

1. According to the viewpoint, what were the numbers of for-profit and community colleges in the top fifteen in the last year of the Montgomery GI Bill?

2. How many students used benefits under the Post-9/11 GI Bill in the 2009–2010 school year, according to Sewall?

3. According to the viewpoint, why is the University of Phoenix so attractive to veterans?

For-profit colleges and community colleges were the most popular choices of students who used benefits from the Post-9/11 GI Bill [Post-9/11 Veterans Educational Assistance Act] this past academic year [2009–10], the first in which the aid was available. The attendance patterns were largely similar to those of students who recently used aid under the previous version of the GI Bill.

Advocates of the post-9/11 bill, which was enacted in 2008, had said it could improve veterans' ability to afford four-year institutions because of its increased benefits and new allowances for housing and textbooks. But data from the Department of Veterans Affairs [VA] show that for-profit and community colleges continue to dominate the list of the top institutions where veterans use their education benefits. Among the 15 institutions that enrolled more than 1,000 students who used the new GI Bill's benefits from October [2009] to May [2010], seven were for-profits and five were community colleges. In 2007, nine of the top 15 under the previous Montgomery GI Bill, as it was called, were for-profits, and three were community colleges.

A total of 270,666 students used the new benefits in 2009–10. Veterans and college officials say cost, convenience, geography, and support systems were significant factors in veterans' college decisions.

The University of Phoenix, whose online-learning program has been particularly attractive to veterans, topped the list, enrolling more than 10,000 students who used the new benefits. Phoenix operates a military division with more than 1,000 employees who specifically assist and advise veterans. It also awarded 50 scholarships to veterans in the 2010 fiscal year, worth $4,000 each, and will increase the maximum amount to $7,000 for next year.

Lamonte W. Mills, a veteran who is a student at Tidewater Community College [TCC], in Virginia, says he returned to the college, which he attended in 2000, because of its low cost and welcoming environment. He felt at home there in part because of the large veteran population and because of the support veterans receive, from "the provost on down."

Tidewater, which has four campuses near the large naval base in Norfolk, enrolled 2,405 students who used Post-9/11 GI [Bill] benefits in 2009–10, the fourth highest total.

Mr. Mills, 29, served in the air force on active duty from 2007 to 2009. When he heard about the expanded GI Bill, he applied for early exit from active duty and is now a member of the air force reserve.

Graduating from college was always a goal of his, he says, and his military experience helped him focus on a plan. Mr. Mills now has his sights set on earning a law degree.

"I was going to apply to various other colleges and universities, but I was led back to TCC," he says. "It feels like home. When I was gone for so long, I wasn't certain if anyone would remember me. But everyone did. They thanked me for serving."

Bigger Benefits

The Post-9/11 GI Bill offers benefits that weren't in the Montgomery GI Bill, an advantage that its sponsors hoped would make four-year colleges more accessible to veterans. Under the Montgomery bill, benefits are adjusted annually, on the basis of average undergraduate tuition. The new GI Bill gives veterans up to the full amount of tuition and fees at the most expensive public college in their states. And it provides a monthly housing allowance and an annual stipend for textbooks.

The new bill also includes a "yellow ribbon" program, which seeks to help veterans attend private colleges, graduate schools, and out-of-state public institutions. The federal government matches the amount of financial aid pledged by participating colleges above the base educational benefits for tuition and fees provided in the new GI Bill. More than 700 colleges and universities participated in the program in the past academic year.

The post-9/11 bill also makes it easier to transfer benefits to a spouse or child.

Israel De La Cruz, who is on active duty in the army, transferred his benefits to his wife, Venetia. She is pursuing a bachelor of science in human services management at the University of Phoenix.

"I wanted to take classes online so I could stay home with my kids," says Ms. De La Cruz, who lives with her husband and two children in Fort Lewis, Wash. "And we put our son's name on the benefits, too, so he'll be able to use them."

The programs of seven of the top 15 colleges enrolling recipients of GI Bill aid are largely online. And many of the 15 operate satellite campuses near military bases.

University of Maryland University College, which ranked third, enrolled more than 3,000 GI Bill recipients over the past academic year, on campuses near U.S. military bases in Europe and Asia, in Maryland, and online. It was one of 20 colleges to receive $100,000 grants last year from the American Council on Education and the Walmart Foundation to increase programs and services for veterans. Maryland has used the money to create an online classroom orientation program and a campus orientation for veterans, as well as to conduct four open houses specifically for veterans.

"We were military-friendly before it became a marketing term," says John F. Jones Jr., the university's vice president for Department of Defense relations. "We've always been so proud of having a large military component among our student body, and the new GI Bill has allowed us to continue serving even more veterans."

Outreach by Four-Year Colleges

Although four-year public colleges are not enrolling as many veterans using GI Bill benefits as are some for-profit and community colleges, a number of them are also increasing efforts to do so, and to improve campus services for them.

Some institutions, such as San Diego State University and the University of Missouri at Columbia, have recently opened offices to provide veteran-specific services. Last month the University of Utah opened the National Center for Veterans Studies, a joint effort of its College of Law and College of Social and Behavioral Science, that will conduct research, provide outreach and vocational training, and engage in nonpartisan advocacy for veterans.

As part of the center, the university also created a National Service Academy, which will tailor some courses to veterans' talents and experiences. Hiram E. Chodosh, dean of law at Utah, says veterans' drive to serve their country could be refocused to service in other areas, like health care and civil engineering.

"One of the ways we're trying to help veterans is by knowing we need veterans to help us," he says. "They represent an incredibly untapped resource of talent and training."

Some public four-year universities are seeing more success than others in enrolling veterans. Arizona State and Ohio

There Is a Role for For-Profit Colleges

For-profit colleges have an important role to play in higher education. The existing capacity of nonprofit and public higher education is insufficient to satisfy the growing demand for higher education, particularly in an era of drastic cutbacks in state funding for higher education. Meanwhile, there has been an enormous growth in nontraditional students. . . .

In theory, for-profit colleges should be well equipped to meet the needs of nontraditional students. They offer the convenience of nearby campus and online locations, a structured approach to course work and the flexibility to stop and start classes quickly and easily. . . .

Many for-profit colleges fail to make the necessary investments in student support services that have been shown to help students succeed in school and afterwards, a deficiency that undoubtedly contributes to high withdrawal rates. . . .

For-profit colleges . . . receive the largest share of military educational benefit programs: 37 percent of Post-9/11 GI Bill benefits and 50 percent of Department of Defense Tuition Assistance benefits flowed to for-profit colleges in the most recent period. Because of the cost of the programs, however, they trained far fewer students than public colleges. Eight of the top 10 recipients of Department of Veterans Affairs Post-9/11 GI Bill funds are for-profit education companies.

US Senate Committee on Health, Education,
Labor and Pensions, "For Profit Higher Education:
The Failure to Safeguard the Federal Investment
and Ensure Student Success," July 30, 2012.

State Universities, for example, enrolled 716 and 548 students, respectively, using Post-9/11 GI Bill benefits in the past academic year.

Both universities were cited by the online 2010 Guide to Military Friendly Schools as being attractive to veterans because of their sheer size and their online programs. Both also offer scholarships specifically for veterans. Campus officials say they have seen an increase in the number of veterans and their family members using the post-9/11 benefits compared with those in the older GI Bill.

Charlene P. Kamani, supervisor for veterans' benefits and certification at Arizona State, says it enrolled about 60 percent more veterans across its campuses this past year than in 2008–9. The new law, she says, "offers them a greater ability to come here."

Further Expansion Sought

The Post-9/11 GI Bill took effect less than a year ago, in August 2009, but a U.S. senator already wants to expand its benefits.

Sen. Daniel K. Akaka, a Hawaii Democrat and an army veteran, introduced legislation last month that would make all members of the National Guard and reserve programs eligible for the new GI Bill benefits. His proposal would allow veterans to receive aid for a wider array of educational programs, including vocational and on-the-job training, and would make it easier for them to qualify for the housing and textbook allowances.

The bill would also base benefits on a national average of tuition, instead of on the highest public college tuition in each state.

"We are excited that there is again movement in making some legislative changes to the new GI Bill," says James Selbe, assistant vice president for lifelong learning at the American Council on Education.

While the bill's prospects are unclear, and its cost has not been estimated, the council continues to focus on ways to improve how colleges serve veterans. Following up on the $2 million in grants that the council and Walmart issued last year to 20 colleges, the council will identify colleges that used the money to create the best programs and will urge other colleges to adopt the most effective practices.

"There's a pretty large-scale effort nationwide in building the capacity to serve veterans," Mr. Selbe says. "But there's still work to do within institutions to improve the veteran experience of transitioning from service to school."

> *"[The Post-9/11 GI Bill has] become a cash cow for for-profit schools ... eager to capitalize on vets coming back from Iraq and Afghanistan."*

For-Profit Colleges Are Taking Advantage of Veterans

Adam Weinstein

Adam Weinstein is a senior writer for Gawker *who also has written for* Mother Jones. *In the following viewpoint, Weinstein argues that for-profit schools, attracted by the government's more generous benefits under the Post-9/11 GI Bill, have been aggressively marketing to veterans. As more federal money became available, the for-profit colleges' share of that money went up dramatically, reports the author. Weinstein says that veterans are advised to seriously look at the claims made by for-profit schools because many employers place little value on degrees from these institutions.*

As you read, consider the following questions:

1. According to the viewpoint, what are some of the ways in which for-profit colleges recruit veterans?

2. What dropout rate does the author cite at the ten for-profit colleges taking in the most Post-9/11 GI Bill cash?

3. According to the author, why are for-profit colleges targeting veterans?

L ast winter [2011], the Department of Veterans Affairs [VA] tasked its newly hired blogger, a cantankerous Iraq vet named Alex Horton, with investigating the website GIBill.com, one of many official-looking links that come up when you Google terms like "GI Bill schools." With names like Armed ForcesEDU.com and UseYourGIBill.us, these sites purport to inform military veterans how to best use their education benefits. In reality, Horton found, they're run by marketing firms hired by for-profit colleges to extol the virtues of high-priced online or evening courses. He concluded that GIBill.com "serves little purpose other than to funnel student veterans and convince them their options for education are limited to their advertisers."

For-Profit Colleges Are Cashing in on GI Bill

The 65-year-old GI Bill is widely credited with transforming post–World War II America by subsidizing vets' college education and fueling the expansion of the middle class. Yet recently, the program has also become a cash cow for for-profit schools like Capella [University], DeVry [University], ITT [Technical Institute], Kaplan [University], and the University of Phoenix, eager to capitalize on vets coming back from Iraq and Afghanistan.

As a beefier Post-9/11 GI Bill [Post-9/11 Veterans Educational Assistance Act] has kicked in, a surge of service members has left the ranks armed with benefits that will cover the full cost of attending public college. In 2009, the for-profits took in almost as much military money as public colleges, even though they enrolled about one-third the number of vets. Spending on military education benefits has shot up to $10 billion; for-profit schools' share of that money has gone up 600 percent, as revealed in a recent PBS *Frontline* exposé. For example, at Kaplan . . . military revenues grew to an estimated $48.9 million last year, up from $2.6 million in 2006.

The result has been a bonanza for schools' executives and shareholders. "We didn't foresee that the for-profit sector, eager to please Wall Street investors, would go after this new funding aggressively, often in ways that are not in the best interests of veterans and service members," stated Sen. Tom Harkin (D-Iowa) after leading an investigation into 30 major for-profits earlier this year. Or as one University of Phoenix alum put it on RipoffReport.com, the school "treats military students like cash piñatas."

Online ads are just the opening salvo in the for-profit schools' recruitment campaign. The 400,000-student University of Phoenix runs a "military division" that employs 600 vets, operates satellite campuses on military bases worldwide, and publishes an online military newsletter called the *Patriot*. The American Forces Network has made an exception to its no-commercials policy to air the school's ads. "We feel putting this information on the air is beneficial to the community," a program director at the network told *Stars and Stripes*. For-profit schools' "military enrollment advisers" are also routinely given access to soldiers on bases. An investigation by Bloomberg found that a recruiter visited Camp Lejeune's Wounded Warrior ward, hoping to enroll injured marines.

For-Profits Provide Little Value at a High Cost

For-profit colleges bill themselves as flexible job-training programs, but their costs can outweigh the benefits. At 8 of the 10 for-profits that take in the most GI Bill cash, more than half of students drop out within a year of matriculation. Many students find that prospective employers and graduate schools

For-Profit Colleges Fail to Meet State Standards

Over the last five years, more than $600 million in college assistance for Iraq and Afghanistan veterans has been spent on California schools so substandard that they have failed to qualify for state financial aid.

As a result, the GI Bill—designed to help veterans live the American dream—is supporting for-profit companies that spend lavishly on marketing but can leave veterans with worthless degrees and few job prospects, the Center for Investigative Reporting found.

"It's not education; I think it's just greed," said David Pace, a 20-year navy veteran who used the GI Bill to obtain a business degree from the University of Phoenix's San Diego campus.

Although taxpayers spent an estimated $50,000 on Pace's education, he has the same blue-collar job he landed right after he left the service: running electrical cable for a defense contractor.

Aaron Glatz, "GI Bill Funds Flow to For-Profit Colleges That Fail State Aid Standards," Center for Investigative Reporting, June 28, 2014.

won't take their course work seriously since most for-profits lack accreditation from legitimate academic bodies. "I researched the accreditation and it seemed legit. I had no idea . . . none of my schooling would transfer," an army vet and University of Phoenix alum from St. Petersburg, Florida, wrote on the VA's GI Bill Facebook page. "A lot of places see the guaranteed GI Bill as cash in hand and it's a shame they take advantage of us."

Some for-profits have cleaned out students' military benefits while also signing them up for thousands of dollars in loans without their knowledge. A vet who enrolled at the largely online Ashford University after being told the GI Bill would cover his tuition ended up owing the school $11,000. "I felt that I have been misled, deceived, or even outright lied to," he told Senate investigators.

At some schools, more than 60 percent of military students ultimately default on their loans. A 2010 VA audit found serious bookkeeping errors at nearly every school it reviewed: An Arizona school didn't give a veteran promised tuition discounts and pocketed $20,000; a New Jersey school collected nearly $5,000 in tuition from a student after he'd been recalled to active duty.

How did this much-loved program become corporate welfare? Congress expanded GI Bill benefits for service members and their spouses just as investors were looking for fast-growing stocks—like educational for-profits—to replace the once hot real estate market. Tuition assistance is now paid directly to institutions, not soldiers, making it easier for schools to convince vets to sign over their benefits. GI Bill dollars have also enabled for-profits to boost how much federal financial aid they receive. In order to collect federal Title IV aid—Pell grants, Stafford loans, and PLUS loans—the schools must obey the "90/10 rule": They can't derive more than 90 percent of their total income from Title IV programs. GI Bill funds don't count toward that total. So every dollar of military aid enables for-profit schools to collect nine dollars from the Department of Education.

The VA oversees the disbursement of GI Bill money, but its bureaucracy has been swamped by the glut of soldiers turned students. It relies heavily on reporting from state agencies, which in turn frequently rely on information cherry-picked by the schools themselves—an approach, the Government Accountability Office notes, that "undermines the independence of the review." Harkin and a cohort of Democratic senators have proposed stricter guidelines for the for-profits, which spent more than $7 million on lobbying last year. The plan has found few additional supporters in Congress.

In the meantime, Horton and his colleagues on the VA's outreach team continue their war on misinformation. "We're not in the business of telling veterans where they can and can't go to school," says his boss and fellow Iraq vet Brandon Friedman. "But we can give vets enough knowledge to make a decision."

Horton encourages service members to do their homework so they get the best value for their benefits. "Take a look at the CEOs and directors of those for-profit schools, Kaplan, DeVry, Ashford. Where'd they go to school? Harvard, Stanford, Oxford," he says. "Zero are for-profit graduates."

Periodical and Internet Sources Bibliography

The following articles have been selected to supplement the diverse views presented in this chapter.

George Altman — "Post-9/11 GI Bill Turns 5," *Navy Times*, August 4, 2014.

Paul Fain — "Follow the Money," *Inside Higher Ed*, July 26, 2013.

Angel Grace Jennings — "Congress Passes Bill to Improve Access to Education for Veterans," *Daily Californian*, August 4, 2014.

Steven Knapp — "Stepping Up: We Must Do More to Help Student Veterans Succeed," *The Presidency*, Spring 2013.

Janet Lorin — "For-Profit Colleges Lead Top Recipients of GI Bill Funds," Bloomberg, July 30, 2014.

Daniel Luzer — "How For-Profit Colleges Target Veterans," *Washington Monthly*, August 2, 2013.

Hollister K. Petraeus — "For-Profit Colleges, Vulnerable G.I.'s," *New York Times*, September 22, 2011.

Alexandra Rice — "Why For-Profit Colleges Target Veterans," *Huffington Post*, June 3, 2014.

Libby Sander — "At Half a Million and Counting, Veterans Cash In on Post-9/11 GI Bill," *Chronicle of Higher Education*, March 11, 2012.

Libby Sander — "Veterans Embrace Post-9/11 GI Bill, but Remain Wary of Its Potential Costs," *Chronicle of Higher Education*, March 26, 2012.

Leo Shane III — "GI Bill Changes Could Send Some Veterans into Deep Debt," *Stars and Stripes*, February 28, 2011.

For Further Discussion

Chapter 1

1. The magazine *G.I. Jobs* argues that most veterans readily find jobs and that stories about their unemployment are exaggerated. In contrast, Andrew Tilghman in *Army Times* writes that veterans returning from Afghanistan and Iraq are struggling to find jobs and have an unemployment rate higher than that of the civilian population. *Army Times* is a general interest publication aimed at active military members and veterans, and *G.I. Jobs* is a magazine specifically aimed at military members transitioning to a civilian career. Both publications are for-profit and not affiliated with the US government. As you read each viewpoint, why do you believe each publication chose its position? What do you feel the unemployment situation is for veterans? Explain your reasoning.

2. Senator Bill Nelson, a Democrat from Florida, supports the Veterans Jobs Corps Act, while Senator Tom Coburn is opposed to it. What reasons does each give for their position regarding the act? With which senator do you agree? Do you believe that their party affiliations have anything to do with their positions? Explain your reasoning.

Chapter 2

1. Cheryl Pellerin quotes Department of Veterans Affairs (VA) undersecretary for health Robert Petzel as saying the VA has decreased the suicide rate for younger veterans who use VA services. *New York Times* columnist Nicholas D. Kristof writes that while the VA has improved its suicide prevention programs, it doesn't do nearly enough. Based on the information in these viewpoints and your own assessment, what more could the VA be doing to prevent veteran suicide? Explain.

2. David Wood writes that while historically the suicide rate for military ranks has been lower than that of civilians, that trend is reversing. What are some of the characteristics of the Afghanistan and Iraq wars and today's society that could play a role in an increased suicide rate for active military members and veterans? Explain your reasoning.

Chapter 3

1. Jamie Reno cites several examples of medical malpractice and wrongful deaths at Department of Veterans Affairs (VA) hospitals and says these are typical of the inadequate care veterans receive at VA hospitals. VA undersecretary for health Robert Petzel reports that VA hospitals received high marks for customer satisfaction on the American Customer Satisfaction Index. How would you explain these disparate views of VA hospitals?

2. Eric K. Shinseki argues in testimony before the Senate in 2012 that VA hospitals provide excellent care. What evidence does Shinseki provide to back up this claim? In light of the scandal that erupted in 2014 over accusations of falsification of medical records at some VA facilities, do you think Shinseki's resignation as VA secretary was warranted? Explain your reasoning.

Chapter 4

1. President Barack Obama commented that the original GI Bill passed after World War II "carried with it a simple promise to all who had served: You pick the school, we'll help pick up the bill" and thus created "the backbone of the largest middle class in history." After reading the viewpoints in this chapter, do you think the Post-9/11 GI Bill can produce the same results as the original GI Bill? Why, or why not? Cite examples from the viewpoints in the chapter to support your answer.

2. Michael Sewall writes that many veterans choose for-profit colleges because these colleges have support systems that meet the needs of veterans. Adam Weinstein accuses for-profit colleges of targeting veterans to gain access to federal money while giving veterans an inferior education. Why do you believe so many veterans choose for-profit colleges? Do you believe veterans are getting value for their educational dollars at such colleges? Explain.

Organizations to Contact

The editors have compiled the following list of organizations concerned with the issues debated in this book. The descriptions are derived from materials provided by the organizations. All have publications or information available for interested readers. The list was compiled on the date of publication of the present volume; the information provided here may change. Be aware that many organizations take several weeks or longer to respond to inquiries, so allow as much time as possible.

American Legion
700 North Pennsylvania Street, PO Box 1055
Indianapolis, IN   46206
(317) 630-1200 • fax: (317) 630-1223
website: www.legion.org

The American Legion is the nation's largest veteran service organization. Founded in 1919, it now has nearly three million members. Politically active in lobbying for the interests of veterans, particularly in the area of pensions and medical benefits, the organization also sponsors volunteer activities and commemorative events honoring veterans. It publishes the *American Legion* magazine and documents on a variety of topics, including veteran education and employment.

American Veterans (AMVETS)
4647 Forbes Boulevard, Lanham, MD   20706
(301) 459-9600 • fax: (301) 459-7924
e-mail: amvets@amvets.org
website: www.amvets.org

For more than sixty years, American Veterans (AMVETS) has continued its objective to assist all veterans, through professional counseling by service officers, legislative lobbying on Capitol Hill, and volunteering at hospitals. There is also strong support and involvement in community service and initiative to improve the lives of local veterans. AMVETS publishes the *American Veteran* magazine and has a membership of approximately 180,000, organized through local posts.

Center for Veterans Issues (CVI)

315 West Court Street, Milwaukee, WI   53212
(414) 345-3917
e-mail: info@cvivet.org
website: www.cvivet.org

The mission of the Center for Veterans Issues (CVI) is to assist veterans in successfully returning to civilian life. The center provides transitional housing to homeless veterans and offers programs dealing with such issues as post-traumatic stress disorder, substance abuse, unemployment, money management struggles, mental health problems, poverty, and educational deficits. CVI publishes news releases and creates videos to advocate for veterans.

Coalition to Salute America's Heroes

552 Fort Evans Road, Suite 300, Leesburg, VA   20176
(703) 291-4605
e-mail: info@saluteheroes.org
website: www.saluteheroes.org

Founded in 2004, the mission of the Coalition to Salute America's Heroes is to help severely wounded veterans and families of Operation Enduring Freedom and Operation Iraqi Freedom recover from their injuries. It publishes the newsletter *Road to Recovery Report*, which features stories about wounded veterans.

Disabled American Veterans (DAV)

3725 Alexandria Pike, Cold Spring, KY   41076
(877) 426-2838
website: www.dav.org

Disabled American Veterans (DAV) is a veteran advocacy and assistance organization whose mission is to assist veterans and their families to access their benefits, advocate in Congress for the interests of veterans, and educate the public about the needs of veterans in their transition to civilian life. The organization publishes *DAV Magazine* and makes copies of its press releases, speeches, and annual reports available to all inquiries.

Iraq and Afghanistan Veterans of America (IAVA)

292 Madison Avenue, 10th Floor, New York, NY   10017

(212) 982-9699 • fax: (212) 982-8645

website: www.iava.org

Iraq and Afghanistan Veterans of America (IAVA) is an association established to advocate on behalf of the troops and veterans of the wars in Iraq and Afghanistan. It seeks to improve veteran health care, address the needs of female veterans, and educate veterans about educational and vocational opportunities. The IAVA website offers op-eds, success stories of veterans, press releases, and speech transcripts, as well as links to recent media appearances of IAVA spokespeople discussing issues relevant to veterans.

National Coalition for Homeless Veterans (NCHV)

333 ¹/₂ Pennsylvania Avenue SE, Washington, DC   20003

(202) 546-1969 • fax: (202) 546-2063

e-mail: info@nchv.org

website: www.nchv.org

The mission of the National Coalition for Homeless Veterans (NCHV) is to end homelessness among veterans by shaping public policy, promoting collaboration, and building the capacity of service providers. NCHV acts as a resource center for a national network of community-based service providers and local, state, and federal agencies to provide emergency and supportive housing, food, health services, job training and placement assistance, legal aid, and other services to veterans. The NCHV publishes an annual report, a monthly e-newsletter, and a variety of guides, brochures, and fact sheets.

US Department of Veterans Affairs (VA)
810 Vermont Avenue, Washington, DC   20420
(800) 273-8255
website: www.va.gov

The US Department of Veterans Affairs (VA) provides patient care and federal benefits to veterans and their dependents. Among the organization's initiatives are eliminating veteran homelessness, improving veteran mental health, and improving the quality of veteran health care. One of the VA's most important responsibilities is the VA health system, which supervises facilities that offer a wide range of medical, surgical, and rehabilitative care for veterans. The VA publishes the magazine *VAnguard*, books, fact sheets, reports, and a variety of other publications.

Veterans for Peace (VFP)
216 South Meramec Avenue, St. Louis, MO   63105
(314) 725-6005 • fax: (314) 227-1981
e-mail: vfp@veteransforpeace.org
website: www.veteransforpeace.org

Veterans for Peace (VFP) is a global organization of military veterans whose mission is to create a culture of peace with the aim of ending all wars. In support of its mission, VFP engages in activities designed to increase public awareness of the costs of war, lobbies the government against intervention in the internal affairs of other nations, and works for the elimination of nuclear weapons. VFP publishes the *Veterans for Peace* newsletter.

Vietnam Veterans of America (VVA)
8719 Colesville Road, Suite 100, Silver Springs, MD   20910
(301) 585-4000
e-mail: communications@vva.org
website: www.vva.org

Vietnam Veterans of America (VVA) was founded in 1978 to promote and support issues important to Vietnam veterans, to create a new identity for Vietnam veterans, and to change public perception of this group of veterans. VVA was responsible for dedicating the Vietnam Veterans Memorial wall in Washington, DC, in 1978. It publishes the *VVA Veteran* and a variety of publications on health and related topics, including "PTSD: What Every Veteran—and Every Veteran's Family—Should Know."

Wounded Warrior Project

1120 G Street NW, Suite 700, Washington, DC   20005
(202) 558-4302 • fax: (202) 898-0301
website: www.woundedwarriorproject.org

The purpose of the Wounded Warrior Project is to raise awareness of the needs of injured veterans, to help injured veterans aid and assist each other, and to provide programs and services to meet the needs of injured veterans. The organization publishes the magazine *After Action Report* as well as brochures, annual reports, and fact sheets.

Bibliography of Books

Michael P. Abrams, Michael Lawrence Faulkner, and Andrea R. Nierenberg
Business Networking for Veterans: A Guidebook for a Successful Transition from the Military to the Civilian Workforce. 2nd ed. Upper Saddle River, NJ: Pearson Education, 2014.

Mark Baird
American Crisis: Veterans' Unemployment. Pleasantville, TN: Inspired Authors Press, 2013.

Robert M. Bossarte
Veteran Suicide: A Public Health Imperative. Washington, DC: American Public Health Association, 2013.

Mark Boulton
Failing Our Veterans: The G.I. Bill and the Vietnam Generation. New York: New York University Press, 2014.

Mathew H. Bradley, ed.
Veterans' Benefits and Care. Hauppauge, NY: Nova Science Publishers, 2010.

Paula J. Caplan
When Johnny and Jane Come Marching Home: How All of Us Can Help Veterans. Cambridge, MA: MIT Press, 2011.

Victoria L. Collier
47 Secret Veterans' Benefits for Seniors—Benefits You Have Earned . . . but Don't Know About! Scottdale, GA: Collier, 2010.

Stephen S. Coughlin — *Post-Traumatic Stress Disorder and Chronic Health Conditions.* Washington, DC: American Public Health Association, 2013.

Patricia P. Driscoll and Celia Straus — *Hidden Battles on Unseen Fronts: Stories of American Soldiers with Traumatic Brain Injury and PTSD.* Drexel Hill, PA: Casemate, 2009.

Sylvia J. Egan, ed. — *Post-Traumatic Stress Disorder (PTSD): Causes, Symptoms, and Treatment.* Hauppauge, NY: Nova Science Publishers, 2010.

Deniz Emre — *Best Boot Forward: A Guide for Transitioning Post-9/11 Veterans.* Boston, MA: Poetic Life Publishing, 2012.

R. Blaine Everson and Charles R. Figley, eds. — *Families Under Fire: Systemic Therapy with Military Families.* New York: Routledge, 2012.

Erin P. Finley — *Fields of Combat: Understanding PTSD Among Veterans of Iraq and Afghanistan.* Ithaca, NY: Cornell University Press, 2011.

Aaron Glantz — *The War Comes Home: Washington's Battle Against America's Veterans.* Berkeley, CA: University of California Press, 2009.

Janelle Hill, Cheryl Lawhorne, and Don Philpott — *The Wounded Warrior Handbook: A Resource Guide for Returning Veterans.* Lanham, MD: Government Institutes, 2009.

Charles W. Hoge *Once a Warrior Always a Warrior: Navigating the Transition from Combat to Home—Including Combat Stress, PTSD, and mTBI*. Guilford, CT: Globe Pequot Press, 2010.

Terry Howell *The Military Advantage: The Military.com Guide to Military and Veterans Benefits*. Annapolis, MD: Naval Institute Press, 2014.

Michelle Tillis Lederman *Heroes Get Hired: How to Use Your Military Experience to Master the Interview*. New York: NBC Publishing, 2013.

Phillip Longman *Best Care Anywhere: Why VA Health Care Is Better than Yours*. Sausalito, CA: PoliPoint Press, 2010.

Bret A. Moore and Walter E. Penk, eds. *Treating PTSD in Military Personnel: A Clinical Handbook*. New York: The Guilford Press, 2011.

Stephen R. Ortiz *Veterans' Policies, Veterans' Politics: New Perspectives on Veterans in the Modern United States*. Gainesville: University Press of Florida, 2012.

Daryl S. Paulson and Stanley Krippner *Haunted by Combat: Understanding PTSD in War Veterans*. Lanham, MD: Rowman & Littlefield, 2010.

Allen Rubin, Eugenia L. Weiss, and Jose E. Coll, eds. *Handbook of Military Social Work*. Hoboken, NJ: John Wiley & Sons, 2013.

Barry R. Schaller   *Veterans on Trial: The Coming Court Battles over PTSD*. Washington, DC: Potomac Books, 2012.

Jacob L. Turner, ed.   *The Post-9/11 GI Bill and Other Veterans Education Assistance Programs*. Hauppauge, NY: Nova Science Publishers, 2013.

Mary Beth Williams and Soili Poijula   *The PTSD Workbook: Simple, Effective Techniques for Overcoming Traumatic Stress Symptoms*. 2nd ed. Oakland, CA: New Harbinger Publications, 2013.

Index

See also GI Bill (1944); Post-
9/11 GI Bill (2008)
Turner, Brian, 161

U

Underemployment, 29–35, 210
Unemployment
  Civil War veterans, 67, 68–69
  federal assistance programs,
    29, 31–32, 34–35, 43, 62–65,
    67, 72
  female veterans, 19, 20
  GI Bill as remedy, 180
  rates, civilian population, 19,
    23–24, 26*t*, 30–31, 43, 71
  rates, veterans, 19, 20, 23, 26*t*,
    30–31, 43, 54
  See also Employment
Unemployment benefits, 24, 25
Ungar, Rick, 55
Uniformed Services Employment
  and Reemployment Rights Act
  (1994), 45
University of Georgia, 182, 185
University of Maryland University
  College, 202–203
University of Missouri, 203
University of North Carolina,
  193–194, 195–197
University of Phoenix, 201, 202,
  208, 209, 210
University of Utah, 203
US Army Corps of Engineers, 61
US Bureau of Labor Statistics
  (BLS)
    education information, 25
    employment data, 19, 23, 24,
      26*t*, 43
US Chamber of Commerce, 72

US Citizenship and Immigration
  Services, 39
US Congress
  federal hiring laws and poli-
    cies, 38, 40–41, 42, 43–52, 72
  for-profit colleges, policies,
    204, 212
  House Veterans' Affairs Com-
    mittee, 87, 100, 137, 138,
    140, 142, 143, 151, 153, 167,
    177, 192, 196–197
  job corps bill criticisms, 58–67
  job corps bill support, 53–57
  Post-9/11GI Bill alteration
    bills, 192, 196–197, 205–206
  Republicans' lack of support
    to veterans, 55, 64
  WWI bonus pay, 69–70, 180
US Department of Agriculture, 61
US Department of Commerce, 61
US Department of Defense
  budget, 34
  hiring, 61
  suicide data, 91, 110
  suicide prevention programs,
    90, 91, 92–93, 96, 101, 104,
    110–111
  Transition Assistance Pro-
    gram, 34
  tuition assistance program, 65,
    204
US Department of Education, 34,
  211
US Department of Homeland Se-
  curity
  hiring, 61
  hiring and careers, 39
US Department of Housing and
  Urban Development, 15
US Department of Justice, 61

W

Y

Z